'James Michel is a pioneer of the Blue Economy. He constantly advances new ways to achieve a healthy and resilient ocean, and we are honoured to count on him as a Pew Bertarelli Ocean Ambassador. Since stepping down as President of the Republic of Seychelles, James Michel has continued to advocate for the Blue Economy, a concept which is now recognized globally as key for long-term sustainable development and for the future of the communities which rely on a healthy ocean. I am delighted that he has highlighted his contribution to the Blue Economy in this, his latest, book, as an inspiration for all of us and to share his valuable legacy.'

Dona Bertarelli, Co-Chair Bertarelli Foundation, Founder Sails of Change

---

'In 2009, as Vice-Chancellor of the University of London, I received an invitation from the then President of Seychelles, James Michel, to visit Seychelles, primarily to discuss his wish to create a University of Seychelles. His vision was inspiring and he very clearly recognized that, even in a small country like Seychelles, investment in education and especially higher education was of lasting benefit. He also made it clear that such investment should be linked to the best quality provision available and his preference was to make use of the long-established external programmes of the University of London. This was not an easy option but, building on available experience in further education, he and his academic team showed very clearly that they could present a range of programmes meeting all the very rigorous requirements of the University of London's quality assessments. The University was established in September 2009 and it has played a key role in transforming Seychelles into a knowledge-based society. The University of Seychelles is indeed an important and masterly part of the legacy of James Michel's presidency.'

Sir Graeme Davies, Emeritus Vice-Chancellor, University of London

---

'James Michel is a visionary; someone with the rare ability to see beyond the horizon while at the same time keeping his feet on the ground, and never losing touch with the people. Three times in this new millennium he was chosen to be his country's president and during his twelve years in State House he achieved great things. Politics, though, is a rough trade and critics may be tempted to rewrite history to suit their own ends. That is why it is important to read what this former leader has to say in his own words. To put the record straight. To remind us how a small island state won a place on the world stage. To reassess the true value of his enduring legacy.'

Emeritus Professor Dennis Hardy, Writer and Academic Consultant

Also by James Alix Michel

A Man of the People: A Collection of Speeches

Distant Horizons: My Reflections

Island Nation in a Global Sea: Making the New Seychelles

Rethinking the Oceans: Towards the Blue Economy

LEGACY

New Millennium, New Seychelles

JAMES ALIX MICHEL

First published 2021
© James Alix Michel 2021

All rights reserved. No part of this publication may be reproduced, stored in a retrieval system, or transmitted, in any form or by any means, electronic, mechanical, photocopying, recording or otherwise, without the prior permission of the publisher.

This book is sold subject to the condition that it shall not, by way of trade or otherwise, be lent, resold, hired out, or otherwise circulated without the publisher's prior consent, in any form of binding or cover other than that in which it is published and without a similar condition including this condition being imposed on the subsequent purchaser.

Enquiries concerning these terms should be addressed to

Blue Gecko Books

bluegeckobooks@ymail.com
www.bluegeckobooks.com

Hardback ISBN:978-0-9575685-3-2
Paperback ISBN:978-0-9575685-4-9

Design and formatting by Barbara Velasco (Papel+Papel Creative)

All photos from the private collection of James Michel

Front cover: James Michel with his daughter, Laeticia

*To my family and friends, whose support has given me strength,
and to the people of Seychelles who have accompanied me on my journey.*

The Tears and Smiles of Time

Countless secrets have I smothered
Yet this one I must reveal.
I am not the one who has always been!
The world that lies before me
Is not the only one I've seen.
On the tails of comets have I travelled,
Suffocated in the hearts of dying stars,
Spat out of supernovas,
Cast into the abyss of distant worlds
And scattered in countless universes.
In far off galaxies have I dined,
On horizons unknown have I stepped and surfed
And learnt the songs of my distant earth.
To angelic melodies have I danced
And endured the nightmares of dark shadows.
Spinning upon Saturn's dusty rings,
And countless nebulas,
I was flung into the pits
And saw the colourless face of oblivion.
I've learnt what makes souls lament and weep;
I've sung celestial lullabies
That caressed the moon to sleep.
From afar, have I contemplated God,
To be both the flowing water
And the extinguishing flame.
I've been frozen, I've been molten,
Been pulverized in the event horizon.
And shall be so again.
And again.
Though I've been a billion things,
This one can smile and cry,
With or without a face,
And feel the caress of time.
I'm the pieces of the universe
In faceless, human form.
For a while ...
Until the inexorable end.

JM

Contents

Prologue		11
Part 1	**My Way**	13
	❖ Odyssey	15
	❖ Truth	37
Part 2	**Through a Glass, Darkly**	109
	❖ Succession	111
	❖ Shadows	129
	❖ Identity	145
	❖ Reflection	169
Part 3	**A Glimpse of the Future**	177
	❖ Recognition	181
	❖ Agenda	189
	❖ Utopia	203
Epilogue		211
Notes and References		213

Prologue

No legacy is so rich as honesty.[1]

For twelve years it was my privilege to serve as the president of Seychelles. I had held ministerial posts in government for many years before and was the country's first vice-president. Throughout a combined period of nearly four decades in political life, I always did my very best to make things better for all the people in our island nation.

My presidency started in 2004 and in three subsequent elections my leadership was endorsed by the people of Seychelles. When I stood down in 2016, I did so out of choice; it was the right time to hand over the reins of power to my deputy, so that he could make his own mark before the presidential election which would take place in 2020.

Obviously, my time in State House was special to me as an individual, but this book is not simply a personal memoir. It is, instead, an opportunity for me to reflect on my time in office and, in my own words, to put on record what I was able to achieve. I have called it 'Legacy' because that is what it describes; something that I was able to pass on to my successor and to my country. When I was in office, I dealt with issues on a day-to-day basis. But I was also looking ahead, making plans for Seychelles in a rapidly changing world.

People may ask why I have left it until now to reflect on this earlier chapter in my life. For me, the time is right. I thought it best to wait until after the 2020 presidential election, and then to let the dust settle. It has not been my intention to interfere in the ongoing business of government nor the democratic process. Apart from the question of timing, there is a gap to be filled in recording the modern history of Seychelles and this book does just that. I want to share the experience of leading the nation in a period of great change – at the start of the present century, at the start of a new millennium. There is, though, an added reason for writing this book now. The fact is that, since I stood down in 2016, certain aspects of my presidency have been the subject of distortions and my character has been questioned. At the very least, it is time to put the record straight.

Although this is a retrospective account I have, as well as looking back, spent long hours thinking about the future. Especially with the impact of the global pandemic, and the changes this has brought to so much of what was previously taken for granted, there is an urgent need to refresh time-worn assumptions. But the future is not created in a vacuum, and I believe that the work I did when I was president laid a sound basis to address the challenges we are presently facing.

There is more to be said about the future, but for now I simply invite you to join me in retracing the steps that brought us to where we are. I care deeply for my nation and I am proud of what was achieved during the period of my presidency. Past, present and future are intertwined; so let me, in this volume, begin to disentangle these different strands.

Part 1

My Way

I planned each charted course
Each careful step along the byway
And more, much more than this, I did it my way.[2]

- ❖ **Odyssey**
- ❖ **Truth**

❖
Odyssey

Odyssey: more than just a journey.[3]

The story I have to tell could not have been imagined. I was born in 1944, and sixty years later I entered the office of President of the Republic of Seychelles. It was a long and, for most of that time, an unexpected journey that took me from the simple surroundings of my childhood to the grandeur of State House. Today, a car will cover the distance between the two places in no more than thirty minutes. But for me the route was far from direct, and certainly not ordained. It was an island journey, not just in terms of geography but in meaning too, for there is something special about islands and those who live on them.

In spite of the hardships she endured, my mother (pictured here with my daughter, Laeticia) has turned 100

It all started on Mahé, one of more than a hundred islands in the Seychelles archipelago that is scattered widely across a remote stretch of the western Indian Ocean. Mahé is the largest of these and the most populated, although by international standards it is small, often shown as a mere dot on the world map. This is where I grew up, on the picturesque west coast, in one of a string of tiny settlements facing the sea. Tourists now come to enjoy the white, sandy beaches fringed by coconut palms and the invariably turquoise waters. In contrast, for those of us who lived there when I was young, this idyllic setting was little more than a backcloth to the daily struggle to put enough food on the table to feed our families. But roots run deep and memories of this early experience remain an important part of what was to follow.

Surrounded by the sea, far from other countries, islanders develop a remarkable resilience to the many challenges that face them. No people show more respect for the sea, yet that creates not fear but a shared determination to survive. Islanders are independent in spirit but also communal, knowing that they have to help each other. Tradition is important but not at the expense of change; as the writer, D.H. Lawrence, conjectured, 'the past is vastly alive, and the future is not separated off'.[4]

In this opening chapter I will recount the story of my own island journey, over the first six decades of my life. Subsequent chapters will recall what I was later able to achieve and pass on as a legacy to the country I love. But the one informs the other and I can see now just how much this earlier experience was, for me, a time of learning and development – in its way, an apprenticeship for my future position. Because of these years of preparation, by the time I became president I was ready and confident to meet the challenges that lay ahead.

Many years passed before I made my momentous step to take up the post that awaited me in State House. In that formative period, so much was changing in the world around me and nothing could any longer be taken for granted. But that was not necessarily evident when I was growing up. I might well have thought as a boy that my future was already mapped out, following the same path that others had taken before me. The bays and beaches of the west coast could well have been where I would stay. Yet nothing was further from the truth and, instead of being constrained by tradition, I found myself constantly adapting to change and anticipating what might come next.

Perhaps it is too easy to be introspective, simply tracing my own development, but the fact is that the second half of the twentieth century was a period of transformation. Like a great wave sweeping across the sea, it was impossible to resist. Indeed, the world changed almost beyond recognition in a matter of decades, more than at any earlier time in human history and, inevitably, this would rub off on my own life. All of our lives are a journey through time, and I am reminded of the work of the science-fiction writer and socialist, H.G. Wells, who, in a different era, raised the idea of time travel. 'There is no difference,' argued Wells, 'between Time and any of the three dimensions of Space except that our consciousness moves along it'.[5] And, as the consciousness of one person is different from that of another, we may each experience time in different ways.

The more I was drawn into politics, the more it seemed that nation and self were inseparable

With the benefit of hindsight, time has been shaped for me by the interaction of two overlapping processes. One is the way my own country was transformed during my lifetime, from its colonial background to an independent nation in which I was personally privileged to play an active role. My own development was deeply affected by this set of events, so much so that I feel in many ways that *nation* and *self* are inseparable. The other process that has powerfully influenced my own development is to be found in the multitude of changes that have transformed the world as a whole. The fact of globalization as an intricate network of connections came into its own and has affected all of our lives. I sometimes reflect on how it was when I was a young boy compared with how it became; even before the impact of the pandemic, it seemed that everything had changed and nothing was any longer as I once knew it.

In the following sections of this chapter, I will say a little more about these inter-related processes – within Seychelles and then globally – to show just how important they have been, but let me first track my own circuitous journey to the presidential office. This will help to explain the ideas and values I would bring with me to the post. I have written elsewhere about this early stage of my life,[6] so suffice to say in this present volume that persistence in the face of adversity is an object lesson of the importance of human will. Even though things were so heavily stacked in favour of the privileged, I somehow found my own way to make a difference. I had never gone in search of power but it was as if a hidden path was suddenly revealed, a path of opportunity.

Retracing Footsteps

As a young boy, I would often walk barefoot along the sandy beach of Anse à la Mouche on Mahé's west coast… I launched my little boat made of coconut husk and looked across the turquoise sea to the distant horizon, wondering what lay beyond.[7]

As I grew up, I would spend a lot of time thinking. I wondered why things were as they had become in my own country, and I wondered what things were like in the rest of the world. What was the same and what was different? Was it an inevitable fact of human development that a few people would always be very rich while most would not? I was eager to discover more about most things and would avidly borrow any book I could find to seek answers. Ideas turned over in my mind, always questioning whether the limits of our existence were necessarily the work of fate. Surely things could be different. What lay beyond those distant horizons I could see from the beach every day?

I made the most of the schooling that was available and am eternally thankful for the help I was given in learning to read and write; that was a great and enduring gift. Beyond a basic level, however, the way was blocked, for only children of parents who could afford to pay the fees were able to receive the kind of education that was necessary to join a profession. Even though I was bright enough to proceed to a higher level, I was prevented from going beyond a few years at secondary school. As a result, career opportunities were limited, although I did the best I could. First, I trained to be a teacher and spent a couple of years in post. Although I enjoyed the experience, in 1962 I joined Cable & Wireless, the largest employer on the island, where I spent the next ten years. I was diligent in my work and enrolled on correspondence courses to improve my skills. At the same time, I could not help thinking a lot about the injustices that surrounded me. I became involved in union activities, urging my fellow workers to campaign for a better wage. This led me, in turn, to a confrontation with management and I decided that it was time for me to move on.

I then worked in the accounts office of a large hotel and was soon promoted to the position of manager. But I could never put out of my mind the kind of injustices I had observed previously in my workplace and, indeed, I could never forget my own experience of being unable to continue with my schooling simply because the fees were beyond the reach of my family. In different ways I came to realize that these concerns could well occupy more of my time. There were others amongst my friends who thought like I did, agreeing that things could not go on indefinitely as they were. Step by step, the attraction of politics grew within me and I could see that the kind of change that was needed would only come about through an organized movement. By 1974 my commitment to social justice was recognized and I was invited onto the Central Committee of the Seychelles People's United Party (SPUP), the political party dedicated to the struggle for national independence. Against this background, when I was later (in 1977) asked to join a small group determined to oust the first president in favour of a socialist regime, I was ready to show my true colours and devote myself wholly to the cause.

Certainly, the political landscape was beginning to change. Prior to independence, ceded by the British in June 1976, different political factions had already started to make their mark, while in the workplace trade unionism raised important issues. But that was nothing compared with what followed. The founding president, Sir James Mancham, enjoyed the endorsement of the departing British, who knighted him in the year of independence. His presidency, however, was short-lived and, just one year after he took office, while he was out of the country on an official visit to London, he was deposed. His place was taken by France Albert René, like Mancham a lawyer by profession but unlike his predecessor a socialist at heart. This was the time of the Cold War and René's socialist agenda won widespread support amongst countries in the Soviet bloc. In many cases, these countries provided Seychelles with much-needed financial help and expertise, as well as scholarships to enable a new generation of young socialists to study abroad. At the same time, the new president was careful to keep open lines of communication and business ties with the United States, while France, too, proved to be a strong supporter of the new regime, gifting a patrol ship and providing intelligence officers. Now that it had to stand on its own feet, the new Republic of Seychelles needed all the friends it could get and became adept at international diplomacy. In fact, charting a course between the interests of East and West became an axiom of foreign policy ever since, a means of survival for a small island state in the rough waters of global politics.

As an advocate of change, I was personally involved in the transfer of power to President René, and I immediately assumed office as a trusted member of the new regime. For the next twenty-seven years I worked assiduously in a variety of ministerial posts, and in time I assumed the newly-created role of vice-president. It was a long apprenticeship and, in the event, perfect training for what was to follow. In working closely with René, I could see first-hand how he dealt with the daily challenges of office; I could see how important it was to keep the ship of state on course for its avowed objectives; and I could see how he handled factional differences within and outside the chamber of government. In due course, there was also the question of navigating a peaceful transition from a single-party system to a multi-party democracy, with a new constitution in 1993 to provide a platform for this next phase of political development.

At the point when I myself became president, this cumulative experience proved to be invaluable. But that was not all and, with the passing of the years since 2004, I have been able to reflect more clearly on what I brought with me to the presidential office. It was not simply the tangible issues of how government works but, no less, the personal qualities that I acquired in the course of my upbringing and career development. Good values, a sense of justice, the importance of loyalty and hard work, and the vision that enabled me to look ahead: these are all qualities that were to help me on my way. Such qualities are not easily learnt but invariably have long roots which reach back to my early development.

I was, for instance, fortunate that good values were ingrained in my family. I was blessed to be surrounded by honest individuals who gave me love and taught me the difference between right and wrong, good and evil. I probably failed to appreciate fully the importance of the simple lessons imparted at the time but they were to stand me in good stead for the rest of my life. With the aid of hindsight, I realize how much I learnt from the everyday example and guidance of my mother and then, for most of my childhood, from another member of our family (on my father's side) who brought me up like her own. While I was always close to my mother, I owe a lasting debt to the dear lady generally known as 'Dada', who, after my father died when I was just a few years old, selflessly took on the role of my guardian. She was like a mother to me and was unsparing in her devotion. With the help of selling coconuts from her tiny plot of land she earned just enough to pay for our upkeep. We were never rich, but poverty is a relative condition, judged not only by how much we could buy but also by how this compared with others around us. In our small community I was privileged to own a pair of shoes when others went without, I wore neatly fitted shirts, and I even owned a hat to wear on Sundays when I was taken to church. By modern standards we were poor, but at the time I could see that we were more fortunate than others in the neighbourhood.

On reflection, I can also see how much, even then, I cared about things that were unfair within and beyond my own community. I grew up amongst poverty and discrimination and would spend the rest of my life fighting to remove what was wrong. I saw suffering amongst my neighbours as a boy, and then in the workplace as a young man. The system struck me always as fundamentally wrong but by no means inevitable, although it saddened me that many people accepted it as simply how things were ordained. I wanted to change that and my commitment to do so was born not of abstract principles but from what I saw around me. It was a fight for social justice, no more nor less. It explains why I was prepared to support regime change and it gave direction to all that I would subsequently work for.

Another characteristic that I have carried forward has been an innate sense of loyalty and determination to do the best job possible. Working hard has come naturally to me and I have stuck firmly to my principles. In the twenty-seven years when I was in government, before I became president, I was steadfastly loyal to my superior and to the common cause of socialism. Obviously, there would be times when I might have wanted to do things differently but that was never a reason for abandoning the trust put in me. President René knew that he could always count on my unstinting support. Loyalty is a quality that I continue to value and I find it hard to understand how it can sometimes be so lightly dismissed by others.

Finally, I have been fortunate in being blessed with an ability to look beyond immediate obstacles and take a long-term view, to look beyond the horizon. Some would call this vision but, whatever it is called, it has proved to be an invaluable attribute. I have always thought deeply about things and spent many hours on my own contemplating just why things were as I found them. Sometimes I would write poetry and let my imagination run its own course. For the first thirty years of my life, I knew that the way society was organized was wrong but at the time there was nothing I could do to change this; since then, it has all been very different.

Eventually, I would become president and I held that position for twelve years. I knew how privileged I was to be in that position and I eagerly used every opportunity to make a difference. It was an eventful period and, when I stepped down in 2016, I felt that I had done my very best to leave the country in good order. I wanted to hand on to my successor policies and practices that could continue to serve Seychelles well. The nature of this legacy had been shaped by what happened before I assumed high office, as well as by what followed. My life was forged in a cauldron of change and mellowed with human values; everything that I managed to accomplish while in State House was a product of this melting pot of experience.

I never forgot my roots, amongst so many good people

The Making of a Nation

There is a heavy leeway to be made up in this Colony before it can be claimed that reasonable social services are provided and that the people as a whole have a reasonable standard of living.[8]

As suggested in the previous section, my personal development has been inseparable from the development of my country. It was a time of groundbreaking change which saw a remote colony become a nation in its own right, and then follow a course which took it in a very different direction from all that had gone before. This close connection between me as an individual and the course of the nation has remained a central theme in my story.

Prior to independence in 1976, Seychelles retained many characteristics that had been evident when the British first took possession of the colony after the Napoleonic Wars. Slavery, of course, had long been eradicated but, with plantations owned mainly by families of French, and also British, descent, and with the majority of the population living in varying degrees of poverty, much about the country bore the hallmarks of the past. And the fragile economy still relied on the export of a limited number of primary products, wholly dependent on the weather, world demand and international market prices, all of which were beyond our direct control.

It might have been thought that the ending of the Second World War – in which many Seychellois volunteers gave their support to the Allies[9] – would have marked a watershed, heralding the start of a new era of development. After all, much was to change elsewhere in the world in the immediate postwar period. But that was not to be the case in Seychelles and, in its first postwar report, the Colonial Office in London painted a somewhat gloomy picture of these distant islands. It was admitted that there was a great deal to be done but 'the crucial question is, what can we afford?'[10] We were very much in the hands of our colonial rulers and the inference in this rhetorical question was not to expect anything too different, which, indeed, is how it turned out in the opening years of the postwar period.

Compared with other places in the British Empire, Seychelles was not a prosperous possession and its requests would not have been high on the list of priorities drawn up in the Colonial Office in London. In the 1940s and for some years beyond, the economy relied on the export of primary products – like copra and cinnamon, patchouli and vanilla, guano and tortoiseshell – just as it had done for generations before.[11] Market prices fluctuated so that there were good years and bad but, in any case, it became increasingly apparent that the amount produced and the value of each of these products was not enough to sustain a growing population. The real value of Seychelles to the colonial rulers lay, not in the plantations but in its location and the safe harbour of Victoria, which allowed ships of the Royal Navy to refuel and undertake minor repairs in the course of their duty to protect important trade routes in the region. In its expansive empire, the attraction of this colony for Britain was primarily as a secure landing point in a remote stretch of the Indian Ocean. The welfare of its people was a secondary consideration. In other words, although it was worth keeping, annual reports show that orders from London urged that unnecessary costs for social reform had to be avoided.

Largely because of their limited economic value, the scattered islands of Seychelles were rarely visited and little known, literally a backwater in a changing world. Their isolation, though, had its own lure and, in no small part because of this, James Cameron, an astute British journalist, wanted to find out for himself what was here. When, on a voyage from India, he arrived in Victoria in 1949, he initially planned a short stay to satisfy his curiosity.

This stay was soon extended as a result of the irregular stops of the steamers that continued on their way to East Africa. He was clearly shocked by what he found, feeling that he had been cast back in time; he commented, caustically, that 'I feel I am constantly on the verge of being given news of the battle of Waterloo'.[12] It was not just how detached it was from the rest of the world but the resultant conservatism of the landowners, the *grands blancs* (predominantly of French descent but also a minority of plantation owners from Britain), who kept things as they wanted and intuitively put a brake on any proposed change. In Cameron's words, 'they were a charming and hospitable people, insulated so long and by such vast distances from every liberal trend, every humanistic development, that their political attitude is almost medieval'.[13]

It never crossed my mind at the time that I might one day be in the presence of the Pope (in this case, Pope Francis)

When Seychelles first became a British colony (ceded from the French) in the early nineteenth century, it was then governed as part of the jurisdiction of Mauritius, only becoming a Crown Colony in its own right in 1901. Yet, in spite of this long period of British control, the culture of the islands remained overwhelmingly French. The original plantation owners were allowed to stay and their influence was buttressed by the powerful hold of the Catholic Church. Although the propertied elite led comfortable lifestyles, the majority of the population, the labouring class (largely of African descent but also the families of previously indentured workers from India) mostly lived in poverty. This was partly because of an unjust system of distribution (itself originating in a period of slavery) but also because the limited resources of the archipelago meant there was only so much to be shared. Although the poorest in society were in a clear majority (with some 30,000 labourers and their families in the 1940s), in the first part of my lifetime they were denied a political voice and there seemed no prospect of material improvement. This, as it transpired, was a situation that could not be expected to last forever.

One way and another, in such a deeply conservative society, for a young man without privilege and money, it seemed that in all directions the way to make a better future was blocked. The *grands blancs* were driven by an over-riding desire to keep the labouring class firmly in its place. Wages were kept to an absolute minimum, while education and health facilities for the workers were seen as a needless expense. To secure their position further, the landowners formed a political party with the apt title of the Seychelles Taxpayers Association (later changed to Planters and Taxpayers Association). The aim, of course, was to pay as little tax as possible.

Albeit with a different set of interests, the Catholic Church was rooted in a conservative doctrine and was even more resistant to change. In many ways, the religious establishment behaved as if nothing had taken place since the eighteenth century; it was almost as if the French Revolution and all that followed had simply passed them by. In the local communities the parish priest was a force in the land, keeping a watchful eye on what people were doing and what the children were taught. Immune to criticism, the Church failed to modernize the education system that it largely controlled. We all attended one class a day on religious instruction (much like we did for other subjects) and participated in the events of holy days, which, given the power of the Church, was not excessive. The real problem was that not all of the teachers were properly trained and were not always fully conversant with the subjects they taught. It has to be said, though, that in spite of the difficulties they faced, the teachers I knew did their utmost to pass on their knowledge and encouragement to young people in their charge. Despite any academic shortcomings they helped us all to understand the importance of good values. For their dedication and basic humanity, I and others of my generation remain eternally grateful.

Finally, most of the colonial governors, appointed by the British, seemed content to leave things much as they found them, due largely to lethargy on their part and a lack of political ambition. Seychelles was an amenable posting for administrators from London nearing the end of their respective careers, and they quickly realized that they were not there to rock the boat. If they tried to do so – and especially if it aroused controversy or exceeded budgets – they could expect a stiff rebuke from senior bureaucrats and politicians in Whitehall. A few notable exceptions were prepared to take the risk of invoking this kind of displeasure, in the interest of limited improvements in key areas like health, wage levels and education. But these efforts, no matter how well-intentioned, invariably fell short of what would have made a real difference to the socially divided colony. In fact, apart from the early ending of slavery, a century and a half of British rule resulted in remarkably little social and material change.

In the world in which I grew up, this was simply how things were. Given the pace of change elsewhere, Seychelles was something of an anachronism, a residual group of islands in the far reaches of the Indian Ocean, left in something of a time warp. For a young Seychellois, it was not a place to excite personal ambition unless, that is, one came from a wealthy family. With so many opportunities out of reach, it is not surprising that successive governors would warn of a potentially unstable situation. They had been content to leave things as they were so long as there was no fear of serious dissent, but now they could see clouds on the horizon. As a result, in the decade before the colony was granted independence, the tone of respective governors' warnings became more urgent; in the words of one report, it was noted that 'a disturbing fact is the wide economic gap which separates the *haves* from the *have nots*'.[14] The message was belated but stark.

Even then, on the eve of independence, there was a sense that much was immovable. But there were cracks in the structure and, just a year after the British left and Seychelles raised its own flag, everything changed almost overnight. With the founding president ousted, the new socialist regime wasted no time in ushering in a different kind of economy, with new systems of education, health, housing and, for the first time, policies to improve the incomes of the long-oppressed labouring class. Seeing the unexpected direction of change, many of the formerly privileged class hurriedly left the country to start new lives elsewhere; in some cases, they were given no choice. But for me, my life took a dramatic turn for the better. No longer was I on the outside looking in but now I found myself at the very heart of government, serving a regime in which I believed. Suddenly, and unexpectedly, the future was to look very different indeed.

I was actively involved in many aspects of the new regime

A World of Change

Today the world is very different, transformed by the digital revolution and advances in medicine and human knowledge. But has it changed in the ways we hoped it would?[15]

After generations of social and economic stagnation, Seychelles changed beyond recognition. But that was not all, for all around us an even more fundamental transformation was taking place. And far from being immune to this we would, inevitably, be caught up in the maelstrom of a changing world.

Although our attention was focused very clearly on events within our own islands, it became ever more obvious that what was happening in the world at large could hardly be ignored; familiar landmarks in human evolution were themselves disappearing. Science and technology were at the heart of it all but, rather like the eruption of a volcano that can trigger a tsunami, far-reaching social and economic repercussions followed. Change in my lifetime has been my constant companion but, as a politician, I have had to be wary, always asking (as the above quote suggests) whether it was necessarily for the good.

When I was born, the world was still engaged in a war that had spread across continents. But, apart from the violence between nations, wars are also renowned for triggering change. Unlike in peacetime, there is no limit to what governments are prepared to spend in pursuit of victory, giving rise to a host of inventions as well as consequent social adjustments. This was especially true in the period during and following the Second World War, largely because of the direct involvement of the United States on its inexorable path to world-leader status. For better or for worse, the Americans cast the mould for the rest of the world, dominating not only in military power but also through ushering in the first consumer society. Capitalism set the pace and in America's determination to succeed in the face of the competing system of communism we were all drawn into the subsequent Cold War, a battle between opposing ideologies, from which America emerged some forty years later as the victor.

Not that the rest of the world allowed this consolidation of power to take place without question. Small nations like my own welcomed the emergence of a non-aligned movement – with nations inspired by Yugoslavia and India, Indonesia and Ghana – which sought to find space between the great powers to assert alternative values. But, of course, nothing is permanent and, with the collapse of the Soviet Union, the Cold War eventually ended. America emerged omnipotent. But new alignments started to form, not least of all in the present century with the rise of China and, more recently, India as rival powers of growing importance. A new geopolitical map was being drawn.

So much has changed in my lifetime and the rate of it all has been relentless. Moreover, it has been exponential, gathering momentum year by year. Many of the new features have unexpected knock-on effects, not all of them beneficial. For all the complexity of this process, however, if one is to think of those things that have had the greatest impact there would be a high degree of consensus.

Who would question, for instance, inclusion of the invention of nuclear weapons, unleashed for the first time in the form of atomic bombs during the Second World War, and changing the nature of international relations forever? Even in my own region, two Indian Ocean nations (India and Pakistan) are nuclear powers while Iran aspires to be one too and China is ever more influential; America, France and Britain also retain active interests in the changing geopolitical map of the Indian Ocean. Never before had the very future of the human race itself been in question. In contrast, the use of nuclear power for peaceful purposes cannot compare to the existential impact of military applications.

Another far-reaching change which dates from that same period is the start of the computer revolution, applied first in military scenarios but later in the century through personal devices and the internet, radically changing everyday lives. If one adds to this the use of mobile phones, it would be hard to disagree with the idea of the present being the Information Age. Instant and global communication has reached into all aspects of government, commerce and personal transactions. People everywhere have access, not simply to information in itself, but to the making of political decisions, while the use of social media has added a new (and not always positive) ingredient to the mix.

Launch of the undersea fibre optic cable at Beau Vallon: from being a remote island, Seychelles now enjoys global connections

Medical breakthroughs have also been evident throughout this period, not least in the near-universal availability of antibiotics. Diseases which once killed millions have been largely eradicated. Covid-19 in 2020 effectively brought the world to a stop but it was not long before a range of vaccines appeared on the market. And, more recently, the science of medical genetics has enabled more personalized forms of treatment. At a simpler but still effective level, better diets and access to a greater variety of foods, if used wisely, are also improving the quality of life. Everywhere, people are living longer, which is all to the good, even though an ageing population gives rise to its own economic and other challenges.

Transport is another field that has brought wide-ranging change. The near-universal use of the automobile has broken the bounds of traditional travel patterns, one effect being, through a new network of journeys to work, to offer greater choice of employment. Likewise, air travel has changed the nature of geographical space, in effect making the world smaller and more accessible. At least prior to the global pandemic which peaked in 2020, geographical isolation is now largely a thing of the past, a fact that is especially meaningful for a previously remote country like my own.

In my own lifetime I have witnessed the first landing on the moon; I have marvelled at the technology of submarines, which have been largely restricted to military use but which can offer so much more to our understanding of the oceans; at home I can switch on a television and find myself connected to events in real time in all parts of the world. As a young man, I remember watching the first aircraft coming in to land on the long runway of what was then our new international airport, ending forever the sense of remoteness that had always been part and parcel of life in Seychelles.

One can add other examples, too, but this list is surely enough to make the point that just about every aspect of our lives has been remade since the middle of the last century. Nor is this all, as this concentration on inventions ignores the resultant social and economic revolutions that are also evident. Partly as a result of medical discoveries, the population of the world has increased from around two billion when I was a boy to the present level of close to eight billion and rising. This in itself adds to problems of food security and access to fresh water, yet the incidence of poverty is being reduced year on year. Nations have won their independence and can now choose their own paths of development. The place of women is still constrained in many parts of the world but in most countries there has been a gender revolution, with women gaining greater access to power. Literacy is no longer the preserve of the few and opportunities for education at all levels have increased.

Of course, these changes are not necessarily universal and progress is measured incrementally, within and between different nations. But, taken together, the world has experienced an amazing journey, taking us to a very different place from the one where we started. By the end of the twentieth century, we were already living in a global society. Once, the limits of my world would have been the shoreline of the island where I was born. Now it stretches in all directions, knowing no boundaries. Nor is this merely the recognition of how things have become, as if that were the end of it. Instead, further change and new challenges continue to arise almost on a daily basis. Some of what is new will bring benefits, while some will create their own problems. But all are deserving of a response; turning one's back on change is not an option. This is a lesson I have learnt through experience and it is why I have embraced globalism with enthusiasm. It explains why, when I became my nation's president, I was able to bring to high office a global perspective; I was already a citizen of the world. In turn, as I will explain in the following chapter, the small island state of Seychelles would soon find a place on the international stage.

One can never forget that the Office of the President is held in trust for all the people of Seychelles

Truth

Great is Truth, and mighty above all things.[16]

Truth has been my constant companion in politics, and nowhere more so than when I was in State House. I was not overawed by my position but I was never without respect for what I was charged to do. The people of Seychelles had put their trust in me and I was wholly committed to repaying them in kind.

In the twelve years when I was president, I never forgot my roots. I recalled the poverty that was all around me when I was a boy, and what it was like to have missed the opportunity of a good education. I never forgot what it was like to see my mother go hungry or to know how hard everyone in our community worked for so little. Yet also I never forgot how people helped each other, with the gift of a fruit or a fish, no matter how poor they were themselves. Nor did I forget how proudly my family maintained good values in the face of adversity. I was more fortunate than many others but life was still a struggle for us all. By 2004 so much had changed since my childhood but these memories were forever in my mind. I cared passionately about justice and finding ways to improve conditions for my fellow citizens. These were thoughts that never left me and drove me forward to do the best I could for my people; these were the foundations for the legacy that I would later pass on.

Of course, at the time I was president, on a day-to-day basis the thought of an eventual legacy was not foremost in my mind. Each day there were matters to attend to and never enough time to deal with everything: Cabinet meetings to chair, ministers with matters to discuss, foreign ambassadors to meet, projects to be launched in the communities, party business to attend to, overseas journeys to be made. My diary was forever full. It was only later, after I decided to stand down, that there has been time to reflect on what I had been able to achieve; it is only now that I can really think of my various actions as adding up to a legacy.

I was in office for long enough to make a difference and I believe I did so on a number of fronts. Of course, there would always be more I wish I could have done. Great progress was made in protecting the environment of our island, but by the time I left office I had not quite reached my goal of 54% protected status. I often thought of the changes that could be made to beautify Victoria and it dismays me to see the indifferent architecture that is now commonplace. Our national university had got off to a good start but was still vulnerable to future policy change. But I have to be realistic and recognize that there were only so many things that could be done in the time. I had to set priorities and I believe I chose the right ones.

Most challenging of all the tasks I faced was the economy, and I duly spent much of my time working not only to avert a potential crisis but also to set things on a new and more sustainable course. Additionally, linking this with my passion for the environment, I worked hard to introduce the idea of the Blue Economy as an essential part of our thinking and actions. At the same time, I never lost sight of the importance of young people, to whom the future belongs, so I was constantly involved in a variety of initiatives for the youth of our country. While I was president, I was also very active on the international stage, winning support to combat piracy in our waters and promoting the interests of small island states, as well as strengthening relations with foreign powers. Finally, there was the question of addressing a range of issues at the heart of what I have termed the New Seychelles and this, too, was constantly on my agenda. Other items had to be dealt with as well but, if asked to say what constituted my legacy,

I would highlight the following:

- reforming the economy, weathering the storm of the Global Financial Crisis and avoiding the dangers of a debt trap;

- working for a sustainable environment, at sea as well as on land, with the Blue Economy central to my thinking;

- supporting and encouraging young people as good citizens and future leaders, free of the debilitating curse of substance abuse;

- taking the interests of Seychelles onto the international stage, while also championing the cause of all small island developing states; and

- setting in place good governance and making the New Seychelles work.

Economic Reform: The Centrepiece of my Legacy

Seychelles' success in executing challenging reforms despite economic uncertainty offers useful lessons to all. These lessons may encourage other countries to embark on ambitious reforms to set, or reset, a similar course toward stability, growth, and long-term sustainability.[17]

Of all my achievements, the one which gives me particular pride is the transformation of the economy. It was both reactive, in responding successfully to a dire economic situation that had been worsening over the years, and proactive, in winning popular support for new policies that would lead to a more sustainable future. I hope that, when my legacy is judged, this will be regarded as the jewel in the crown, the most precious of all of my main endowments. In my own mind it certainly is, not least of all because it was a result of government by the people as well as government of the people. Without the changes introduced then, and without popular support, Seychelles would not be in the sound economic position it was by the time I left office.

Unsustainable budgets

One year after independence, under the leadership of President René, the new Republic of Seychelles followed an avowedly socialist path, initially in the form of one-party rule. I have already explained (in the previous chapter) why I supported this radical turn of events. For all of its earlier history, the country had been sharply divided into the 'haves' and 'have nots', a structure that the colonial power was content to leave as it was and which the first president showed no sign of addressing. There was some tinkering at the edges but the basic division remained intact. So, when the coup happened, in 1977, I was very much on the side of change; and when a new government was formed, I was proud from the outset to play my part by taking on ministerial responsibilities.

At the heart of the changes that followed was a new model for the economy. In contrast with the past, priority was now to be given to resources to pay for free education and healthcare, for social welfare and subsidized housing for those in need, and for good public services. And working conditions had to be improved for all. These changes, I believe, were necessary if we were to redress the gross imbalances of the past. But where was the money to come from to pay for it all? Being very heavily dependent on imports for most of our needs, and with limited exports, an ample supply of foreign exchange was essential. Yet that was always in short supply and, as a result, borrowing became a key feature of the government. Without addressing the root cause of the shortage, the problem persisted in the ensuing years.

Foreign investment was urgently needed but, at the time of the establishment of the new regime, there was remarkably little in the way of infrastructure to support new economic development. An important exception was the long landing strip on Mahé, constructed by the British and operational for military aircraft from 1971. The motive at the time was to enhance security in the region, but the airport would later underpin the growth of tourism, which soon became the main source of foreign income. Additionally, because it was the period of the Cold War, countries in the communist bloc were willing to provide generous grants for infrastructure, education and training opportunities for young Seychellois to study abroad. Russia and the Soviet bloc countries led the way in offering material support. As part of their aid, skilled labour from those countries was seconded to work here in fields like healthcare. Because we constantly feared an externally motivated attack on our young regime, or even an internal rebellion, we needed training and equipment to defend ourselves, and were reliant on overseas assistance for this as well.

As a low-income economy at that time, we were eligible to apply for other forms of international aid too, and we negotiated loans to help us on our way. These various, external subsidies were invaluable at the time but to some extent they obscured the fact that the economy was not sustainable in the long term; at some point it would become apparent that Seychelles was spending more than it earned and that we could not rely indefinitely on the support of friends. Debts were growing and there was no obvious way they could be repaid.

More than a quarter of a century later, by the time I entered State House as the country's third president, this gloomy prognosis of impending debt had for some years become a harsh reality. The situation had been allowed to drift and, not to put too fine a point on it, the country was on the verge of bankruptcy. This was no secret and everyone in the country was aware of constant shortages in the shops, a result of insufficient foreign exchange for traders to buy even basic commodities. From around the start of this century, it was known as the era of *napa* ('there is nothing'),[18] the words uttered by shopkeepers in response to requests for most products. The cupboard was bare.

It must be remembered that I came into office part way into the mandate of the outgoing president, with two years before a general election was due. I knew that only then, if I were successful at the polls, would I be free to act in my own right. In those first two years, I used to see the former president on a regular basis and it was clear that he did not share my sense of a need for drastic measures to deal with the ailing economy. More than that, he was vehemently opposed to taking external advice (from global finance agencies) that would interfere with his own preference for continuing with deficit budgets into the foreseeable future. He and I differed strongly on this point, as I was convinced that we had to find a more sustainable way of managing the economy. I argued that more of the same would no longer work but I believe that the former president never changed his view that I was wrong to pursue this alternative course of action.

By the time, in 2006, when I obtained my own mandate from the people, the situation had worsened but at least then I felt free to start the process that was long overdue. Borrowing had reached an unsustainable level and this inhibited our ability to invest as we needed to. Deficit budgets had served their purpose in providing for the people who had for so long previously been neglected, but for how long could we continue to run our economy on the basis of debt? If all that we had achieved since colonial times was not to be lost, urgent action had to be taken.

Remaking the economy

Under the banner of the 'New Seychelles', I set to work. No-one appreciates the achievements of my former mentor, France Albert René, more than I do; after all, his presidency saw an improvement in the GDP and an increase in personal incomes that far exceeded those of other African countries. In his twenty-seven years at the helm he brought about previously unimaginable changes. But the economy was not sustainable and it was undoubtedly time to do things differently; it was time to restructure and liberalize the economy in a way that had not, under the previous regime, been on the agenda. Towards these ends, and with the help and advice of certain multilateral institutions and bilateral partners, I launched the Seychelles Macroeconomic Reform Programme. As a means to encourage inward investment, one of its major components was the devaluation of the rupee; with our currency at the time pegged at an artificially high level, there was little incentive for foreigners to enter the market.

Although I knew that devaluation would not be a popular move, especially amongst those with large deposits of rupees, it was something which would best serve the interests of the country as a whole. Being popular with everyone was not an option and, in any case, my priority was to do what was best for the ordinary people of Seychelles. To avoid what would certainly have been a run on the banks, I announced the launch of the reform programme in a televised address to the nation on the evening of 31 October 2006. With the following day, All Saints Day, being a public holiday in Seychelles, the banks would be closed, which gave time for a measured response when they reopened. A run on the banks was the last thing the country needed.

Devaluation was a big step in itself but I knew that this alone could be no more than a short-term palliative. It had to be part of an overarching strategy for the economy and a series of related measures was needed. In fact, external events were to force the pace and we no longer had the luxury of concentrating on our own problems in isolation. Shortly after embarking on our own reforms, the world economy was shaken by the onset, in 2008, of the Global Financial Crisis. We were inevitably swept into the whirlpool but, as it happened, we soon found that our initial preparations had not been in vain; on the contrary, we were in a much stronger position to withstand the global crisis than if we had not given prior thought to economic sustainability. Our position was strengthened by the fact that we were already in discussion with international experts, through the auspices of the IMF and the World Bank, which together were in the business of advising and assisting ailing economies.[19] Their shared motive was not primarily one of altruism but rather of ensuring stability in the world economy; our motives might have been different but there was an essential synergy in the relationship.

I could personally see the benefits of calling in international experts but not everyone agreed that it was the right thing to do, the former president and his own advisers included. Critics drew attention to an established pattern of intervention by bodies like the World Bank, especially in Africa, which amounted to restricting expenditure until income could be increased. In one sense this made perfect economic sense, but in Seychelles, given all that we had done to alleviate poverty and improve conditions for our people, there was a limit to what we would be willing to cut back. In particular, the maintenance of free education and healthcare for all was non-negotiable, as indeed were other social benefits. We would adopt a responsible approach, reducing expenditure in other areas, but we would not cast away those prized gains that had brought unquestionable benefits to our people. That was our immovable stance. In response, there was, at first, scepticism amongst the international experts and a fear that this position would impede success. But we were convinced that we could make it work and would not give ground.

Even with our precondition to protect essential services, the extent of reforms anticipated was far-reaching: calling for further devaluation prior to floating the rupee on the international foreign exchange market, reducing the role of government in the business of the nation, and encouraging free enterprise. No-one could underestimate the possible risks involved but I was convinced that anything less would be insufficient; we were beyond the point of partial solutions. In economic terms, this amounted to a radically new direction for the country. Yet such a decision could not be made on economic grounds alone; whether it would work or not would depend, no less, on political considerations. Would the people be willing to abandon the essentially socialist approach that had served us well for more than three decades, and would they be willing to make short-term sacrifices in the interests of an unproven economic future? This amounted to an enormous political challenge that, more than anything else, would define my time as president. It was a calculated political risk and, had I failed, I am sure that I would not have been re-elected at the next presidential election. As I have written elsewhere:

> *I knew I had to put political considerations aside and place the future of my country above everything else. I was aware that I was taking a massive political gamble, but I was prepared to do it because I was convinced that it was not only the right thing to do but also the only option to extract Seychelles from the crisis. I knew that the people of Seychelles needed a major change in mindset, to move away from a cycle of economic dependency and reliance on government social services to a new attitude of 'get up and do something for yourself' – 'leve debrouye', as we say in Creole.*[20]

Asking the people

It is hard to overstate the importance of being well prepared to make the necessary changes, even before the advent of the Global Financial Crisis added a new dimension to our existing economic problems. At this point, with the benefit of shrewd advice from the Secretary-General in the President's Office in State House, I arranged to go directly to the people to explain what had to be done and to seek their support.[21] My other advisers and some ministers strongly counselled me not to do so. They all knew that the announcement of strict measures to reform the economy would not be welcomed, even if such changes could be seen to be essential. But it had to be done and I was prepared to take the flak. Honest leadership is not simply about imparting good news but also about having the courage to stand before the people in times of adversity. Fortunately, shortly after I became president, I had toured the districts and, as a result, people already knew me. This bond with the electorate undoubtedly helped me win a new mandate in the presidential election of 2006 and it was to count again now, in the face of our new challenge.

Consultation with the people underpinned the success of our economic reform programme

So the stage was set, and in the first half of 2008 meetings were arranged in each of the administrative districts, which I chaired in the company of my team of ministers. The Leader of the Opposition was invited to join me but refused to do so and an empty chair on the platform signified his decision. I believe that, in political terms, his absence worked in my favour as it could be construed that he was not prepared to put the country first. Perhaps understandably, the first two or three meetings were quite difficult; people were not used to being asked for their thoughts in this way and could not be sure if their involvement was anything more than tokenism. But word quickly spread and, once there was confidence in the process, the whole mood of the meetings changed, from one of cautious interventions to a genuine sharing of ideas. I urged the people to take ownership of the process, for us all to make sacrifices in the interests of the country. It is my firm belief that the subsequent reforms would not have been effective without the strong support and understanding of the people. We all knew that the medicine would be bitter but we also knew that it was our best chance for a full recovery.

I was also heartened by the endorsement of a need for change from my team of ministers, not least of all Danny Faure, who in this crucial period was Minister of Finance and was central to the discussions. It was also important that officials from the World Bank and the International Monetary Fund were onside as well. We all worked closely together to steer the ship of state through rough waters. By the time we emerged from this ordeal, the Seychelles economy was looking very different. The rupee, following a 40% devaluation prior to being floated on the open market, was more realistically priced and sounder as a result. Fiscal measures were tightened and attention was directed to building financial reserves. Fewer people were working in government offices and more in the private sector, with a corresponding shift in mindset from one of dependence on the state as the sole provider. Yet we had also been able to protect our key goals of free education and healthcare, coupled with other forms of support for the poorest in society.

Inward investment started to flow into the country and for this we were especially indebted to our friends in the United Arab Emirates. As well as a substantial donation from Abu Dhabi when our foreign reserves were at their lowest point, the rulers of that kingdom also invested in a number of projects that would bring immediate as well as long-term benefits. His Highness Sheikh Khalifa bin Zayed Al Nahyan, President of the UAE, took a personal interest in our nation and has been a constant source of support. So, too, a special relationship was formed with His Highness Sheikh Mohamed bin Zayed Al Nahyan, who took responsibility over the years to ensure that funding was provided on a regular basis to assist the development of Seychelles. Additionally, we were indebted to the international body, the Paris Club, and other creditors for writing off some of our loans as well as assisting us in restructuring the rest; France played a leading role in supporting these negotiations and we were also helped by South Africa.

The remarkable outcome is not only that we achieved the essential changes we were seeking but (and largely because of the reforms) we survived the worst of the Global Financial Crisis, emerging stronger and sooner than many other nations. In the words of Makhtar Diop, Vice-President of the Africa Region World Bank Group:

> *In a record three years, Seychelles fixed its economic fundamentals, secured generous debt relief from the Paris Club and other private creditors, and today enjoys rapid – and likely sustained – growth.*[22]

We had averted a crisis and were altogether in a stronger position than before. Indeed, we were the envy of many larger nations that took longer to overcome the difficulties of the Global Financial Crisis. I take great pride in being at the helm during that challenging period and I could subsequently see how well the new economic regime held up. In the last of my State of the Nation Addresses, in early 2016, I could report that in the past year there had been a growth rate in the economy of 4.34% and the foreign exchange reserve in the Central Bank was US$ 536 million (sufficient to enable almost five months' worth of imports). Through judicious negotiations we were also able to reduce the total stock of our external debts, enabling us to service the remaining stock through regular payments. By the time I left office we had cut the total debt stock to 62% of our Gross National Product and were well on track to reduce this further. All of this was a far cry from the situation I inherited in 2004, when we were on the verge of bankruptcy. As a result, I could hold my head high when, later in 2016, I handed on this healthy state of affairs to my successor.

Sustainable Development: Our Debt to the Environment

Talcum-powder beaches lapped by topaz waters, lush hills, a sublime laid-back tempo; these dreams of a tropical paradise become reality in the Seychelles.[23]

Tourist companies and visitors alike compete for superlatives to describe the beauty of Seychelles. Far from the nearest landmass, enjoying the clean air of the surrounding ocean, the archipelago is home to a natural environment and a relaxed lifestyle that is fast disappearing from the rest of the world. Little wonder it is frequently described as paradise.

Tourism is the mainstay of our economy and visitors are attracted by the prospect of the best that nature has to offer; as such, we have a responsibility to ensure that the environment retains its unique qualities. But we do this for another reason too – because this is our heritage and we value it for what it means to us as a nation. It is an integral part of us as Seychellois – our culture is inseparable from where we live. For both reasons, economic and cultural, governments have an enduring responsibility to protect what we have inherited and to prevent irreversible harm. We should be prepared to say 'no' to any new development that is not sustainable; we must be able to enjoy the environment now but also to ensure that we can pass it on, intact, to future generations. This is our duty. Paradise is a gift to the world; it must also be our national legacy.

Starting with green

It is more than thirty years since a former Norwegian Prime Minister, Gro Harlem Bruntland, chaired a United Nations Commission that in its report highlighted the idea of sustainable development. At that time, the concept was not an everyday term but it was simple to understand and soon became widely known.

> *Sustainable development is development that meets the needs of the present without compromising the ability of future generations to meet their own needs.*[24]

Against a background of growing concern about the deteriorating state of the world's environment, the report explained in a nutshell what needed to be done if future generations were not to be disadvantaged. Sustainability became a global watchword and the concept was soon to underpin policies in nations across the world.

Fortunately, even before the Bruntland Report, Seychelles already had a good reputation for maintaining a balance between development and conservation and we continue to benefit from these earlier efforts. Throughout my presidency I was ever-watchful of environmental matters and lent whatever support I could, not only to maintain but also to enhance new measures and projects that would advance the goals of sustainability. As a result of our consistent history of valuing the environment, we can boast what is truly an enviable record of achievement:

> *Given the uniqueness and the paramount importance of our biodiversity, Government has set aside almost 50% of its land*

territory as protected area. It has over 80% of its land forested comprising mostly of natural forests and plantations established for commercial purposes. About 90% of the forests are natural with plantations covering about 4,800 ha.[25]

Additionally, on the islands of Praslin and La Digue, which are the second and third most populous islands, I introduced a ban on further development above a height of fifty metres. As a sign of what was to come, hardly had I stepped down from office in 2016 than my successor scrapped this limit, thus allowing construction again on the higher (and usually more visible) slopes.

Event to mark the protection of Silhouette Island as a Protected Marine Park

Our various efforts attracted widespread praise from a variety of sources, such as the following appreciation of our consistency of approach:

The admirable conservation efforts of the Seychelles have been ongoing for many years, with work over the last few decades really stepping up to meet the challenge. In fact, more than 40 percent of the overall land mass has now been designated as national parks, ensuring that the huge selection of indigenous flora (more than 250 native plant species) and fauna will survive for future generations to enjoy.[26]

An effective way of ensuring that we would continue to make progress was through adopting initiatives and frameworks provided by international bodies, notably the United Nations. In this way, an important landmark (which I was quick to recognize) dates from September 2015, when world leaders gave support to the UN Sustainable Development Agenda. Of the seventeen goals, one was focused wholly on the land while another concentrated on the overlapping issue of climate change. Goal 15 included the sustainable management of forests and a halt to biodiversity loss, both issues of extreme importance to Seychelles and ones where we could demonstrate good progress to date. But one can never be complacent and, from time to time, specific issues would arise to test our resolve; in those cases, I would sometimes see it as important to personally intervene.

One such issue arose in response to a proposal for the development of a major resort at the beautiful location of Cap Ternay, towards the northern tip of Mahé, bounded by the Morne Seychellois National Park and Baie Ternay Marine Park. Because of the exceptional environment, the creation of the proposed resort was a contentious issue from the outset, when it was first announced in 2007. Certainly, it would have brought valuable foreign investment to Seychelles, not to mention more jobs and subsidiary benefits. The site had previously been used for one of the nation's two residential youth camps during the socialist era but had since been abandoned and was largely overgrown. When the idea was originally mooted, I had in my mind that the development would be on a modest scale, largely within the footprint of the former youth camp. However, when plans were prepared it was clear that the developer envisaged something very much larger, in the form of a US$ 253 million project to provide 400 rooms for guests. It would clearly not sit easily in the landscape, with its requirement amongst other things for extensive dredging in the marine park and irreparable damage to the coral and other marine species, together with the impact of new transport arrangements to connect it to the rest of Mahé.

Such proposals are always subject to a detailed environmental impact analysis but, although the developers offered to reduce the scale of the project, the weight of scientific evidence was against it. I thought this was sufficiently important to demonstrate our consistent stance in protecting the environment and I used my National Day Address in June 2016 to settle the issue once and for all:

> *We always follow the same principle. I have listened, consulted and studied the reports. All the scientific arguments suggest that such a project will affect the environment of the area. Naturally, as the President of this country, it is my duty and responsibility to take the best decision in the interest of the Seychellois people, and for the protection of our heritage. I have decided that there will be no such project at Cap Ternay.*[27]

I endorsed this decision with the addition of a general announcement that planning permission should not be granted for any further large hotel complexes. In the interests of sustainability, we should keep within the boundaries of those resorts that already existed as well as others already approved but not yet built. Limiting the number of large developments in this way would serve not only to protect the environment but would also favour small businesses in the tourism industry.

The future is blue

In devoting detailed attention to the land, I was, in one sense, simply continuing in the footsteps of my predecessor, President René, who had also recognized the importance of the environment during his own term of office. At the same time, I believed we were failing to do the same for the sea. This might sound strange, given that we are an oceanic state, but it seemed to me that over the years we had somehow taken that for granted. It was as if the riches of the marine environment would be there for the taking for as long as we wished. The reality, of course, was that we were in danger of causing irreversible damage to this invaluable resource. If we allowed the exploitation of the sea to continue unhindered (by other nations as well as our own) it would undoubtedly harm the marine environment. If, however, we could manage the process sustainably, there would be valuable resources to harvest, for future generations as well as our own. This is why (during my presidency and after) I laid so much emphasis on the Blue Economy as a keystone for the future of the nation and as a new priority for the world as a whole.[28] It would benefit not only my own nation or even other small island states in isolation: 'a Blue Economy not only empowers island states but can empower us all'.[29]

In short, the intention of the Blue Economy is to make better use of the world's all-embracing ocean. Of course, people have used the sea for fishing and shipping for time immemorial but in most cases this use has been very restricted, ignoring all the other possibilities it has to offer. The Blue Economy must be all-embracing in its approach, recognizing the potential for new activities as well as traditional ones. But an even more important difference from how it has been used in the past is to introduce the idea of sustainability, to ensure that we can pass on the benefits of the ocean to future generations. Exploitation of marine resources without any thought for tomorrow is no longer acceptable; without sustainability there can be no Blue Economy, just as the Green Economy is based on the same principle.

I would take every opportunity to promote the Blue Economy, speaking at high-level conferences and through my book on the subject (in this instance, presenting a copy to leading American environmental scientist and marine ecologist, Jane Lubchenco)

The idea is straightforward and its very simplicity and universal potential is itself part of the attraction, not least of all for countries like my own. Seychelles is an archipelago with a limited land area but is surrounded by a vast stretch of ocean; in fact, the immediately adjoining territorial waters and the much larger Exclusive Economic Zone (EEZ) beyond extend over nearly 1.4 million square kilometres. In most respects, therefore, Seychelles is a large oceanic state and this is surely a source of enormous economic wealth. Yet, like most nations, the sea has, historically, been marginalized, of secondary importance to the land. That can no longer be the case, neither for Seychelles nor for the world as a whole; a new future for our shared ocean has become a matter of global importance.

Because of the need to get the economy on an even keel, the focus in the first half of my presidency was, inevitably, on that priority. But, as the country started to recover and we could again look forward, I was able to devote more time to other issues. The prospect of a Blue Economy had for long aroused my imagination and at last I had the opportunity to see how it could be developed. Not only was it something I cared for in environmental terms but, having confronted the fragility of our economy, I knew it could be at the very heart of the new order.

I was certainly not the first to be thinking of a sustainable future for our seas and I could soon see the basis for a political alliance.[30] Small island states were especially supportive and, working with others, an important turning point came in 2012 at the United Nations Rio+20 Conference. The event was held to enable the world community to continue discussions about the institutional framework for sustainable development in general, and to explore more fully the potential of the Green Economy in particular. While supporting these main themes, representatives of island nations also saw this as a chance to bring the still-evolving concept of the Blue Economy into the same world arena. Arguments were marshalled in a pre-conference report, 'Green Economy in a Blue World', and three basic principles were proposed: the ocean's great resources should be used sustainably, economic benefits should be distributed fairly, and the carbon footprint of the maritime states should be reduced.

Protection of the ocean is a priority not only for now but for future generations

Significantly, in the immediate aftermath of Rio – and as a result of the compelling arguments pressed home by those nations with most at stake in the surrounding oceans – the United Nations produced a Blue Economy concept paper of its own. The message within it was clear, with member nations urged to adopt more sustainable policies for all aspects of ocean governance and development. It was acknowledged in the paper that:

> *Coastal and island developing countries have remained at the forefront of this Blue Economy advocacy, recognizing that the oceans have a major role to play in humanity's future and that the Blue Economy offers an approach to sustainable development better suited to their circumstances, constraints and challenges.*[31]

Getting the imprimatur of the United Nations was a real game-changer, demonstrating that this was no longer for a minority of nations but for the world as a whole. I have argued elsewhere that, as all of the world's continents are surrounded by sea, we are all, in effect, islanders now, including those nations which are otherwise landlocked.[32] The future of the ocean is of urgent concern for us all. To make the point, I realized that, as well as taking the message to international gatherings, I should start to make the changes at home. Seychelles was in an ideal position to demonstrate how the Blue Economy might work in practice and the kind of value it could create. On reflection, I wish that more could have been done during my presidency to integrate the Blue Economy more fully into the life of the nation, but I am still proud of what we managed to achieve in the time.

For a start, one action I took as president was to create a separate government department for the exclusive development and management of the Blue Economy. Even though it was a small department, it helped to ensure that all of the ministries incorporated the Blue Economy in their own thinking. In principle, it is a concept that belongs to us all although in practice it will take much longer before it is fully embedded in the minds of all ministers and the workings of government. My successor continued this initiative and for the first two years it answered directly to the vice-president, before being transferred to the Secretary of State for Foreign Affairs.

Another initiative is based on a recognition that the governance of the ocean remains weak and that nations can do more to fill the vacuum. We all have our own marine boundaries but these are mostly lines on a map, invisible to the eye. Thus, Seychelles has secured a unique agreement with its southern neighbour, Mauritius, to jointly care for and develop the submerged feature known as the Mascarene Plateau, which connects our two nations. Launched in 2012, Mauritius and Seychelles undertook to jointly manage some 400,000 square kilometres of seabed. There is the possibility of extracting natural gas and oil from this continental shelf and, if that occurs, both parties want it to be done responsibly. Even since the two nations first discussed this, research into mineral extraction beneath the sea has advanced, revealing ominous signs of the permanent damage it can cause. To proceed with extreme caution must be the watchword for the future. For now, though, the very fact that two nations are willing to work together in this way is a source of encouragement and an example that others might wish to follow.

A further way of getting the Blue Economy to work comes with the need to attract sufficient investment to fund projects. Government funding would always be limited, while adequate commercial returns are themselves dependent on initial investment from the private sector. As a result, I explored other ways to raise money and was able to broker a unique deal, known as the Debt-to-Adaptation Swap – whereby repayment of an international debt of US$27.3 million was cancelled in exchange for our investment in Blue Economy measures. We would have had to spend the money in any case in repaying the debt, but investing in the ocean is a more rewarding process for everyone. Through this mechanism, for instance, we were able to fund an innovative exercise in marine planning, as explained next.

The then President of France, François Hollande, played a key part in facilitating the debt transfer scheme

Although most countries have a land-use planning system, the use of the sea is too often left to chance. Because of the geography of our archipelago, Seychelles has a very extensive area of designated waters, and this is now the subject of a plan designed to achieve a balance between conservation and development. Following extensive consultation with stakeholders, a marine development plan is being prepared to distinguish between areas where fishing and other activities can be maintained, and extensive reserves that will either be protected as they are or become subject to partial regulation. The main goal is for 30% of the territorial sea and EEZ to be zoned as high and medium biodiversity protection areas. There will be 'no go' areas to provide a natural breeding ground for fish where stocks have been depleted and also to be a sanctuary for biodiversity. Seychelles has already attracted international attention for the progress it is making in seeking to protect 30% of its waters in this way. In due course, I would receive various international awards and recognition of my part in promoting this pioneering work.

When I met The Prince of Wales in Sri Lanka, he supported my idea for Blue Bonds to finance ocean improvements

A further example of a local initiative is through our plan to issue Blue Bonds, a device that is based on the well-tried international example of Green Bonds. This came about as a result of a meeting in 2013, where I was invited by The Prince of Wales to explore the idea further with his Foundation. Guaranteed by government and supported by international financial institutions, this offers a means of attracting private-sector funding through public-private partnerships. The first issue of our ten-year sovereign bonds was designed to fund improvements in the management of fisheries across the Mahé Plateau, an area that is close to our main island and most of the nation's population. It offers the prospect of a classic 'win-win' outcome, repaying investors while at the same time increasing fishing yields.

Finally, I was indebted to The Commonwealth of Nations for providing expertise and funding to enable the production of a 'road map' to set targets and guide the implementation of Blue Economy measures in Seychelles. The work was commissioned and started in my time in office and was then continued under the auspices of my successor.

To make any of the above projects work, an essential requirement is that the seas are safe and there is freedom of movement. At one stage, because of incidents of piracy in the western Indian Ocean that was not the case, and in a later section (on proactive diplomacy) I will show how we dealt with that particular problem. Taken together, I have illustrated how one small nation can make a difference. Other nations are innovating, too, and there is scope for many more to make their own contribution. The possibilities are as extensive as the oceans themselves. Beyond the horizon there is infinite potential to do more. The future is indeed blue.

As this record of a visit to the Great Barrier Reef indicates, my commitment to the Blue Economy was at an international level

Clouds on the horizon

Green and blue, blue and green. We have been hard at work in trying to remake the relationship between sea and land, binding it together with the help of the essential strand of sustainability. But, although our attention was rightly focused in this way, we could hardly ignore the presence of gathering clouds on the horizon; distant from us at first but now very clear. The threat that emerged is, of course, the global phenomenon of climate change.

In fact, land, sea and climate are inter-related issues that affect the world as a whole. With the slow melting of the polar ice caps, sea levels will rise and low-lying islands and coastal plains will be in danger of disappearing. Similarly, with higher temperatures across the planet, the ecology of the oceans will itself be transformed; we can already see the effects on once-vibrant coral reefs but this is only the start. Extreme weather conditions that occur today also provide a preview of things to come. Climate change is an existential threat to life on earth and I was in the vanguard of those who not only warned of what was to come but who urged that immediate action be taken by all nations. Setting an example, I announced measures in Seychelles designed to more effectively conserve water and develop, at least in a limited way to start with, local use of wind power. Immediately, I received a generous contribution from the UAE to fund a project to harness wind energy for the people of Seychelles.

At the beginning of the present decade the international momentum for positive action was fast gathering pace, even though it was already too late to expect that climate change could be stopped. But if a sufficient number of nations were willing to act to reduce the rate of global warming, the extent of change could still be checked. Some parts of the world would suffer the effects more than others but this could never be seen as a local problem; the world as a whole had to take note. As such, I took every opportunity to argue the case of Seychelles overseas and to press for collective action. For instance, on a working visit to France in 2014 I spoke in direct terms of the effects that could already be seen:

> *I am very fearful because climate change is a reality. It is not only something that we are witnessing ourselves but the scientific community has given enough evidence to show that the climate is changing, the planet is warming and the sea level is rising... we see our coast being eroded, we see the migration of fish, the bleaching of our corals, and all these are having adverse effects on our economy, on our people, on our livelihood. It is a reality. We see it every day, we live it every day and we have also been stressing that the world must do something about this.[33]*

Extreme weather conditions are becoming more common, affecting our lives in different ways

The need to respond to climate change is an immediate issue

Recognition of the problem was becoming more evident by the day and it was a priority for me to seize the moment. Following the high-profile exposure of these ideas at an event (explained later in this chapter) organized by the United Nations in Samoa in 2014, a few months later, at the invitation of the Secretary-General of the United Nations, I travelled to New York to discuss with him different ways forward. During that visit, I was selected by the Secretary-General to represent all small island developing states at a dinner with the major powers to plan a strategy leading to the next international conference, to be held in Paris in 2015.

By then the world was alert to the scale and imminence of the problem and, under the auspices of the United Nations, the Paris conference was a momentous event, leading for the first time to binding support for tangible measures. Notably, it was agreed to cut greenhouse gas emissions in order to keep the increase in global average temperature this century to well below 2° centigrade more than pre-industrial levels, and as close as possible to 1.5° centigrade. There was also a commitment to help vulnerable nations adapt to the various impacts of change. Especially as a result of the withdrawal from the agreement of the United States, under the Trump Administration (which set back that nation's commitment by four years), it remains to be seen whether these already challenging targets will be met. At least, with a change of president in 2021, the incoming Biden Administration lost no time in returning to the will of the international community.

Even without the United States at the time, it was important for other nations to keep up the pressure. A notable example of this was our initiative to hold Blue Economy Summits in Abu Dhabi, co-hosted with the UAE. The idea originated in discussions with one of my senior ministers, Jean-Paul Adam, when we recognized the importance of gathering wider support for the concept. Fortunately, our approach to the Crown Prince of Abu Dhabi, Sheikh Mohamed bin Zayed Al Nahyan, was well received. He suggested that an event be held biennially, to coincide on each occasion with the annual 'future energy' conference that he already organized. Under the banner of 'One Ocean, One Future', I was able use the international platform to stress the importance of the ocean for the long-term development of all nations. The occasion was also an opportunity to reaffirm a common commitment to the UN's Sustainable Development Goal 14: to 'conserve and sustainably use the oceans, seas and marine resources for sustainable development'.

It remains a difficult road ahead but I believe I was right to argue as I did in the international arena and, as I will explain later, I continue to do so now although I am no longer president. This has not been a matter of political expediency but an enduring conviction that action must be taken.

Having Faith in Young People

I have absolute faith in the youth of our country. We need to continue to empower our youth – whether it be through promoting entrepreneurship and business creation, or through multiplying the opportunities for education and self-improvement.[34]

I have always had faith in young people. For one thing, I find their company inspiring, unconstrained by the conventions that experience and standing in society too often impose on our thinking. Even (or perhaps especially) very young children can sometimes get straight to the heart of the matter, asking why we put up with one problem or another and why we don't do things in different ways. There is a directness which is appealing in itself, untarnished by lengthy discussions in committees or political discourse. But there is another reason, too, why I value the company and ideas of young people and that is, quite simply, because the future will be theirs. We can do no better than to create opportunities for tomorrow's citizens, tomorrow's leaders. Indeed, can there be any more valuable legacy than to do just that?

This is why, when I had the chance to do so as president, I put in place a number of projects that represent investments in the young, surely the best investments of all. I created schemes to train tomorrow's leaders, I lent support for ways to raise the profile of sport in the country, and I initiated and became the first Chancellor of the nation's own university. I also took on the role of Patron for a new charity for young people, the Jj Spirit Foundation, and I was active in helping to acquire purpose-built accommodation for it, and offering support in other ways too. These were all achievements of which I remain proud. But I would be disingenuous if I were not also to acknowledge that many young people are unable to take advantage of what is available, held back by a range of social issues that have not yet been overcome. As a result, I did my best to bring these to the fore and to encourage fresh thinking in the search for solutions. There are two sides to the moon, one dark the other bright, and we must take account of both to appreciate the whole.

Our own university

Particularly with a small population, it is literally the case that every person counts. Larger nations can afford to take a more global view of their human capacity but we are denied that luxury. In a small country, an individual can make a real difference and so each and every person must be regarded as having an important contribution to make. And it is just as important that individuals are good citizens, upholding the values of the country, as well as acquiring the generic skills to become potential leaders. In the interests of the future of Seychelles, we must create opportunities for all.

One example of this was the idea of forming our own university. This was, in so many respects, a real 'game-changer'. Throughout the tenure of my predecessor, France Albert René, education at all levels had ranked high in government priorities. Attention was rightly placed at first on schools and a polytechnic, and (to provide professional support for teachers) our own teacher training establishment. Meanwhile, with no facility in the country for higher education, students wishing to progress to that level were supported through government funding to study overseas.

The latter was a generous scheme and Seychelles benefited when graduates returned with skills and an international perspective that could be put to good use. But, as numbers aspiring to higher education increased, there were two drawbacks to the arrangement. One was, quite simply, that it was expensive to maintain as it was not only the cost of fees that was covered but also travel and living costs in the destination country. Even more costly was the fact that, in spite of a system of bonding students to work in Seychelles on their return for a specified period, some students remained in their newly-adopted country while others returned for the allotted period but left at the first opportunity. Either way, there was a 'brain drain' which the country could ill afford.

Those were negative reasons for reviewing the situation but I could also see a positive outcome if we were to launch our own university. The important thing was that the nation could then boast its own place of advanced learning, a bold sign that we were serious about the planned transition to become a knowledge economy. Not only that, but a local university would enable many potential students, unable to leave their homes and families to go overseas, to study in their own country.

It was a radical proposal, first announced in my National Day Address in June 2007:

> *We have reached the stage in our development where we have to take bold and daring decisions to take Seychelles and the Seychellois to the next level. The times have changed from when we said that Seychelles was too small to have a university. Our Seychelles may be small in size, but we have grown. We have grown in maturity, we have grown as a people, and we have grown in our capacity. Today, we resolve to develop this capacity further. We will set up a foundation to create a Seychelles university. The foundation will comprise local and international partners to develop a high-level institution of training for Seychellois, as well as foreigners. Our university will develop centres of excellence, for example, for studies in the environment, tourism, maritime and financial services sectors. This is what I want to achieve for the people of Seychelles. This is my wish for our people. I call on all our people to rally behind this cause. Young people of Seychelles, this is the future I am offering you!*[35]

Just two years later the idea became a reality and the first students were admitted to the University of Seychelles. A lot was achieved in a short time to make this happen and for this I am especially indebted to Rolph Payet for his invaluable contribution. It was fitting that, in turn, he should become the university's first Vice-Chancellor.

Of course, along the way there were those who thought the population of Seychelles was too small to support its own university and that it could never work. But we pressed ahead and I knew that, step by step, it would prove its worth many times over. Of course, like other institutions in Seychelles, it would be a small university but that need not be a disadvantage. Working with established partners overseas we could provide a credible range of academic programmes, as well as concentrating on key areas of research aligned to our own national interests. As time went on, we would improve the quality of our main campus and welcome students from overseas. This would not only bring in foreign revenue but an international mix would be of enormous benefit to our local students. I had every confidence that it would work and from the outset I assumed the honorary position of Chancellor.

Indeed, it was as Chancellor that in November 2010 I hosted the formal opening of the university, in the presence of Her Royal Highness, the Princess Royal, Princess Anne. This prestigious occasion was an opportunity for me to affirm the reasons for the university's establishment and, I hoped, to encourage every Seychellois to have pride in the venture. It was, after all, truly democratic in intent, designed for 'students from all walks of life, from whatever background and age… the University of the people'. The future was a knowledge-based society and 'the engine for this transformation is the University of Seychelles'.[36]

In my address on the occasion of the inauguration, I could proudly proclaim that:

> *Our university is a demonstration of our determination as a nation. It is a reflection of our vision to provide equal opportunities to all our*

people. It was a promise that I made when I assumed the presidency, that I will steer our country to a new phase of development that will bring more progress: development that will continue to defend the principles of social justice and equal opportunity for all our citizens; development that will continue to create the conditions that will foster the development of our youth. Our university is here. Our students are here. Together, we are ready for the future.[37]

In the company of The Princess Royal, who came to Seychelles for the inauguration of our own university

Young leaders

A second initiative of which I am especially proud was the launch of a Young Leaders programme, designed to nurture the skills and support the aspirations of a selection of outstanding young people who were already showing the potential to be tomorrow's leaders. The scheme allowed for an annual cohort of around twenty-five students to take time out from their regular jobs to work towards the attainment of a Master's degree. Designed and taught in collaboration with an overseas university, it was a varied programme in which the major part comprised academic classes and assignments. But it also included an overseas placement to enable a comparative perspective on examples of good practice. Additionally, there was an important strand that focused on citizenship and the institutions of government in Seychelles.

The annual graduation event was always a proud moment for all concerned and a time to endorse the value of what had been achieved. Thus, at one of these events I praised the achievements of the graduates and, in the interests of the nation, urged them to go from strength to strength:

> *In the overall context of the country's ongoing and future development, this cadre of future leaders, who have acquired new knowledge, skills and leadership training experiences, represents a significant addition of quality human resources to vital areas of our public and private sectors. The progress already made by so many of these young leaders since their formal graduation from the programme is indeed gratifying, and a solid endorsement of the programme's value. It augurs well for the ongoing and future development of the social, economic and cultural development of the country. It also testifies to the opportunities available to the youth of Seychelles and is a constant reminder to them to make good use of the resources that we put at their disposal… We expect you to be the leaders of change Positive change for the New Seychelles.*[38]

Each year, there were more applicants than places available, a sure sign of the growing interest in the programme. By the time I stood down as president, there had been five cohorts that had successfully completed the programme, a total of some 100 individuals in a position to advance to the next level of their various careers. In a small country, 100 aspiring leaders can make a real difference. I remain convinced that it was a wise investment and who can say what contribution these graduates are already making to the life of the nation? Sadly, however, like other aspects of my legacy – seemingly for no other reason than that the idea was attributed to me – this undoubtedly successful scheme has since been abandoned.

Leadership, of course, is not confined to any one sector, which is why I was keen to extend this kind of opportunity to other areas of life in Seychelles. We rely, day by day, on the professionalism and dedication of our police and military services and it seemed only natural to offer comparable opportunities to young recruits in these sectors too. We need good leadership there, just as much as in the higher echelons of government and commerce.

On the first day of January of each new year, I would address members of the police and defence forces, acknowledging their vital contribution in the past year and looking confidently towards the next. When I did this at the start of 2010, we were all aware of the incidence of piracy in our seas and so the prospect of giving support to bring forward future leaders in these vital sectors was well received. I explained on that occasion that the first cohort of the generic leadership programme had already graduated and that, as well as continuing with that, I was keen to see the same kind of opportunity on offer to the police and military. Rather than seek to copy what already existed, the new programme would be tailored specifically to the needs of those charged with the duty of upholding the law and defending our shores.

I had no doubt of the importance of the initiative and I shared my thoughts with the first cohorts, a total of nearly fifty from the two services:

> *The Police and the Military are the guardians of our freedom. They are the sentinels that ensure our progress and prosperity can continue unhindered by strife, criminality or external threats. As future leaders of these forces, you are in a unique position to*

shape our country's future. Through your motivation and diligence, I know we are in good hands.[39]

A sporting chance

Finally, I can point to a third initiative that recognized the enormous potential of young people. In opening new vistas, education and training would certainly play a big part, but there are other areas of activity too, not least of all sport. Not so long ago, to engage in sport was something of a luxury, available to only a privileged few. Most young people would have spent all of their time at work and helping to support their families, and there was certainly no money to spend on essential equipment. This kind of situation has changed beyond recognition so that sport is now one of the most important pillars of any society, including our own. In a world where sedentary lifestyles, processed foods and the use of motorized transport have led to health problems never before envisaged, sport is increasingly seen as a way to keep the human body fit and well. It has also become a source of economic wellbeing, as an income-generating activity, and an industry in its own right. And, whether competitive or not, sport offers physical relief and an outlet to release everyday tensions. An increase in sporting activities in one's own country is a universal trend but this has been accompanied by a remarkable upsurge in international events, where young people interact in the common arena of football or athletics, swimming or tennis.

For all these reasons, I have enthusiastically lent my personal support to sporting activities, within Seychelles and in friendly competition with the young from other nations. Indeed, a highlight of my presidency was to witness the opening in August 2011 of the 8th Indian Ocean Island Games. Eighteen years had passed since the previous time when Seychelles hosted the tournament, and since then the importance of these events in the island nations of the Indian Ocean had greatly increased. It was a proud moment, all the more so as the decision to do this had not been easily won. When the decision was taken to make the necessary investment, Seychelles was in the throes of making radical changes to the economy and, at the same time, facing the daily threat of piracy. Inevitably, there were those who counselled that we should take a step back but my view was quite the opposite; the very fact that we were facing problems of this magnitude was in itself a good reason to go ahead. Sometimes the right thing to do is to confront adversity head-on, confirming to the world that our sights are set on a bold future and we would not be distracted from this. And how better to do so than to reaffirm our confidence in youth, not only the young people of Seychelles but also those of our Indian Ocean neighbours? As a result, the Games were a great success and I believe we would have let down our young people had we not proceeded.

Opportunities for all

Sadly, not all young people are able or willing to take advantage of the opportunities before them. I was only too aware that a sizeable number remained on the margins of society, failing to make their own contribution and growing up dependent on the goodwill of others. Seychelles needs good citizens yet there were too many who were unlikely to make the grade. This was a problem that could not be ignored. It was not in the interests of those who were already in that situation, and it was certainly not in the interests of the nation as a whole. The problem had first to be acknowledged, prior to taking action.

With a new mandate from the people following the presidential election in 2011, I used my inauguration speech to announce my intention to engage on a programme of moral, social and spiritual renaissance. It would involve all parts of society although I directed most of my attention to young people, where too many lives were so obviously being wasted. In some respects, this kind of problem was not unique to Seychelles but was becoming endemic in modern societies across the world, with traditional safeguards and support mechanisms eroded in the face of far-reaching change. Family and community structures no longer offered the supportive framework they once did; material values loomed larger in the minds of young people than the time-honoured importance of truth and integrity, diligence and loyalty; while respect for leaders and established institutions everywhere seemed to count for less. In the face of this kind of change, young people were in many countries becoming especially vulnerable to a range of social ills, from drug addiction to prostitution, from alcoholism to violence, and from truancy to self-imposed unemployment. It was becoming a universal problem and yet there were no easy solutions. We could learn from experience overseas but I knew that, in any case, we had to find answers that would reflect our own circumstances. Seychelles has its own history, its own geography and its own situation as a small island state, and these would all have a bearing on its present ills.

Just a month after being re-elected, I formally launched the new programme:

> *The message is clear: we have to take actions to redress the wrongs in our society. We need a moral and social renaissance. We need a clean Seychelles. All of us are Seychellois, all of us who live in Seychelles, we have to get our society back on track; we have to clean up. Together.*[40]

I knew that the task ahead of us would not be easy; there would be no miraculous cure. Instead, it would be a long, hard journey, with a multitude of partners jointly chipping away at the various manifestations of decay that hindered progress. I called on good parents who keep a close eye on their children and are intolerant of bad habits; on grandparents who have always played a supportive role and could continue to do so; on neighbours who can help to create a harmonious setting for all their children; on the many professionals who come into contact with children on a daily basis and who do their very best to set them on the right path;

on religious organizations and the voluntary sector for the part they can play; and on every person of goodwill who could contribute in one way or another towards making our society a better one.

For all the difficulties that lay ahead, I remained optimistic that we possessed the will to overcome even the most formidable of problems. I constantly reminded people that we had the advantage of starting from a very strong base, a generally harmonious society with an undeniable sense of pride in our nation. We had achieved so much since our independence and should take heart from this as we faced fresh challenges. Nothing would change overnight but if we were persistent and kept our sights on a better Seychelles we would succeed. For the sake of our children and, indeed, the very future of our nation, we could not contemplate failure. 'Renaissance' means 'rebirth' and we should accept nothing less; there could be no rest until we witnessed the appearance of fresh shoots. From these would emerge the New Seychelles.

Speaking up for Seychelles

Seychelles has achieved a significant reputation as a noticeable player on the diplomatic stage of international politics.[41]

During the twelve years of my presidency, I seized every opportunity to make the voice of Seychelles heard in the international community. This was not a question of self-seeking publicity but because there were issues that could only be resolved with external assistance. Moreover, there were some issues where we could offer a unique contribution. The fact that Seychelles is a small nation could not be allowed to stand in the way of this. We had to project our voice and attract the attention of other nations far and wide; we had to create our own role on the world stage.

Sometimes it is external events which force the pace. Thus, there were two instances when I knew that we had to raise our game and boldly become a global player. One was in response to the outbreak of piracy off the coast of Somalia, which was seriously threatening our national integrity. And the other was to work with other small nations to ensure that our joint interests were not overlooked; together we had to press the case for sustainable policies for the oceans and for constructive resistance to climate change.

The sea as a free and open highway

Modern-day piracy off the shores of Seychelles was largely unexpected. In the minds of many people, piracy belongs to the past and popular images portray the buccaneers of old as colourful, even romantic, characters. Indeed, some of the history of Seychelles is itself bound up with stories of pirates seeking shelter in the many bays around the islands and burying chests of treasure for later retrieval. But, as recent events were to show, piracy is anything but romantic. Instead, it is a criminal activity that can cost lives as well as cause financial and other hardships for victims of these illegal acts. In the case of Seychelles, it cut directly into the core of life in an otherwise peaceful nation.

For years, the former colony of Somalia (most of it previously ruled by Italy, and a smaller section in the north by the British) had been a far-from-stable neighbour in the region.[42] A period of dictatorship kept the lid on for more than two decades but was unable to resolve centuries-old factional differences. When strong leadership gave way to an ineffectual system of power-sharing, the result was a long period of civil war dominated by the various clans. Not only was it to become a zone of political and humanitarian crises but after 9/11 the Americans targeted the country as a breeding ground for international terrorism. It was, in all respects, a failed state where authority had broken down and organized crime was gaining ground. One aspect of this lawlessness took the form of piracy.

Somalia has the longest coastline on the African mainland (some 3000 kilometres in length) and most of it is largely undeveloped. But out to sea are some of the busiest shipping lanes in the world and it was this lethal combination of an absence of authority, organized crime, the despair of young people who could not find legitimate employment, and the lure of valuable cargoes within reach, that led to a level of criminal activity that became an international issue. In fact, although there were incidents of piracy before that, 'it was first recognized in 2008 after the hijackings of World Food Programme vessels'.[43]

Although Somalia is not an immediate neighbour of Seychelles and the focus of pirate activity took place further north, especially in the Gulf of Aden where oil tankers and other ships headed for the Suez Canal, for Seychelles the threat of piracy was quickly seen as a matter of crucial importance. Pirates were soon encroaching into our own waters, putting fishermen at risk in the hope of extracting large ransoms. They were also intercepting container and other shipping bringing essential supplies to Seychelles and – as a result of the cost of ransoms, higher insurance premiums, and extra security arrangements – raising the price of goods coming into the country. It was estimated at the time when activity was at its peak that the additional costs resulting from piracy amounted to some 4% of our nation's GDP.[44] Even tourism, the main source of income for Seychelles, was not immune, with the presence of pirates deterring visitors from sailing in what were previously safe waters.

I immediately recognized that, although Seychelles was especially vulnerable, the problem was too big for our own forces to handle alone; the response had to be at an international level. In any case, it was clear that other nations were starting to be affected as well, not least of all through the threat to regular oil supplies from the Gulf and the important shipping routes southwards, passing the Cape en route for the Americas and Europe.

Our friends within the region and beyond provided vital support – through the donation of essential vehicles and equipment, joint patrols, training programmes and rescue operations – and for this we were very grateful. France was quick to come to our aid and other nations too offered early assistance: five patrol boats from the UAE, one patrol boat each from India and China, and a Rapid Intervention Craft from the UK. But the scale of the problem was escalating and we had to match it with yet more help from overseas, driven by the goal of making the trade routes of the Indian Ocean safe again. It was against this background that, in November 2011, I sent a personal letter to world leaders, urging greater support for what had I termed 'a war against piracy'. I laid emphasis on the need to rebuild the troubled state of Somalia and to defeat the indigenous terrorist group, Al Shabab, but I also called for assistance in strengthening the naval capacity of frontline states like my own.

The response was encouraging and early in 2012 I travelled to London to attend an international conference on Somalia, convened by the then UK Prime Minister, David Cameron. This offered a unique opportunity to put our case before an audience of heads of state and other influential individuals, and in a series of interviews with the world's media I was able to explain not only the predicament of Seychelles but also the part we could play in breaking the deadlock. As an example, in speaking to CNN, I explained the centrality of our role:

> *I have placed an emphasis on Seychelles becoming the anti-piracy hub for our international allies, who are committed to the fight against piracy. It is important to note that the anti-piracy action off the Horn of Africa, as well as the wider Indian Ocean, has been the largest and first international operation of its kind, where the navies of the world's major powers – the US, Russia, China, India and the EU nations – are all working together to combat this security threat.*[45]

During my visit to London to present the case for anti-piracy measures, I met the British Prime Minister, David Cameron

I was granted an audience with Her Majesty the Queen

During my time in London I had a personal meeting with David Cameron and, in turn, he arranged an audience for me to meet Her Majesty the Queen. Then, accompanied by my Foreign Minister, Jean Paul Adam, I was able to meet Hilary Clinton and to put the case for American support.

Delegates at the London conference were all agreed that piracy was a symptom of a failed state where internal controls were non-existent, rather than simply being isolated actions at sea. Until Somalia could control its own borders there was little hope that the problem would recede. In the meantime, actions had to be taken to resist continuing acts of aggression. At last, the international community accepted that words were not enough and that an existing mechanism, offered through an earlier UN Resolution, should now be brought into life. In fact, the mechanism in question had been largely dormant since 2009 but that was now to change:

> *The Contact Group on Piracy off the Coast of Somalia (CGPCS) was created on January 14, 2009 pursuant to UN Security Council Resolution 1851. This voluntary, ad hoc international forum brings together countries, organizations, and industry groups with an interest in combating piracy. Participants seek to coordinate political, military, industry, and non-governmental efforts to bring an end to piracy off the coast of Somalia and to ensure that pirates are brought to justice… Nearly 80 countries and several international organizations participate in the Contact Group, including the African Union, the Arab League, the European Union, the International Maritime Organization, the North Atlantic Treaty Organization, and various departments and agencies of the United Nations.*[46]

This represented a powerful alliance and the full force of a united approach was to have a dramatic impact. Combined operations were planned and navies flying various flags worked together to rid the affected waters of piracy. So successful was the approach that by 2016 there were no reported incidents in the region. However, that did not mean that the pirates had gone away; intelligence suggested that any relaxation of effort would be followed by a fresh outbreak of activity. Indeed, in early 2017 there were reports of a new wave of incidents in that same segment of the Indian Ocean. Containment is an expensive and not entirely foolproof operation but, until Somalia can control its own subversive forces, there seems no alternative but to continue on the same lines. A failed state does not make a good neighbour.

Every cloud, it is said, has a silver lining, and, for all the evils of this episode, there are important messages for the rest of the world. One is quite simply that Seychelles, albeit a small nation, values above all its hard-won freedom and independence and will defend its rights to the last. Another lesson is that it remains a friend of all and an enemy of none; it is at war with the pirates, not the people of Somalia as a whole. And a third message is that no nation is too small to be heard on the world stage and, when there is a need, our voice will carry as strongly as that of any other.

In reflecting on what we achieved in countering piracy I have, correctly I believe, concentrated on national and international interventions. But personal values, too, cannot be ignored and, while I worked hard in formal situations, I never lost sight of what it all meant to individuals on the front line. When, for instance, I met a group of Seychellois hostages on their return from captivity in Somalia I could see how much they had been affected by their experience. Being forced to live in primitive conditions, inimical to their health, and not knowing whether their lives would be spared, had left them badly scarred. Confronted with the reality of the situation I pledged that I would do everything within my power to prevent this happening to any more of my countrymen. And it was not long before my resolve was to be seriously tested. One particular incident at the time illustrates this well and, in a personal memoir that I made to record the event, I have described what happened:

> *To take up the story, Somalian pirates had sailed deep into Seychelles' waters and taken hostage a group of our fishermen who had been legitimately going about their business. The pirates were using a traditional dhow as the mother boat, from which they released a number of skiffs. By the time news reached me, our fishermen had been captured and imprisoned on the dhow, which was by then heading back in the direction of Somalia. From our own coastguard control room, I immediately commissioned our main patrol boat to follow in the wake of the dhow and for a surveillance aircraft to mark the course. The support of some of our special forces (TAZAR) was also enlisted. Through loud-hailers from our patrol boat, contact was established but the Somalians refused to negotiate.*
>
> *Meanwhile, the distance from our own coastline was lengthening and Somalia was getting closer. These were crucial factors, as I was determined that our fishermen should not be incarcerated on the mainland where their lives would be put even more at risk. If anything was to be done, time was of the essence. Any action had to be taken before our patrol boat passed its fuel limit and before nightfall. There was only a matter of hours in which to intervene. Thoughts of a military raid were cautioned by the threat of the captors to shoot our fishermen if an attack was made.*
>
> *I spent the day in the control room with key individuals when someone reminded us that an identical dhow was already in our possession, having been requisitioned as a result of an illegal fishing incident. With the assistance of the captain, we were able to identify the structure and compartments of this kind of vessel. Of particular interest was the location of the fuel tanks as, in the event of firing on the boat, we could not risk an explosion which would*

take the lives of our own people. It was by then the middle of the afternoon and there was little time left to act. With the clock ticking I made a decision to sink the dhow. This required precision shooting from our coastguards to avoid the fuel tanks yet, at the same time, be directed with pinpoint accuracy to create enough holes just below the water line so that the boat would very quickly be destabilized. And it rested on an important assumption that the pirates would be so shaken by events that their own instinct for survival would be to jump into the sea even before they could carry out their threat of killing our own fishermen. Both things had to happen with absolute precision for the plan to succeed.

It was a very high-risk operation and I had no illusions about how tragic it would be if it failed. Everything had to be meticulously coordinated. But, if we were to rescue our countrymen, I could see no other option. To maximize its effectiveness our patrol boat increased its speed and turned into the path of the oncoming dhow. Before the pirates could work out how best to react, shots were fired into the hull of the boat. The shots were accurate and water immediately poured into the vessel, which quickly became unstable. Just as we had expected, the crew immediately jumped into the water to save their own lives. With our captured fishermen also on the deck (having been put there at gunpoint) they were able to make their own leap to safety. The coastguards wasted no time in pulling them from the water before going back to retrieve the Somalian crew, a few of whom had been injured. Fortunately, there were no fatalities on either side and our fishermen were brought safely to shore.

TRUTH

The arrival home of our fishermen from captivity by pirates from Somalia was a moment of great emotion and relief

I have included this in some detail because the events remain firmly lodged in my mind and it illustrates the type of problem we were facing. People often think that leadership is an abstract quality but it is also about personal commitment and practical involvement. It was necessary for me to take sole command throughout the operation and to use my military experience to the full. I have always cared passionately for my people and, as this story illustrates, would go to any lengths to give my support. The fact remains that, whether at a personal or national level, our various actions in combating piracy were to win the praise of international observers; we consistently responded to the challenge as well as we could. As an example of how others see us, I can cite the evidence to be found in two recent academic publications. In one, it is noted that 'Seychelles has acquired a voice in international affairs incommensurate with its minute population and limited resources'; in the other, our efforts were described in the article as 'creole diplomacy', countering the handicap of its limited resources with a smart approach to international relations. This supports my own long-held belief that Seychelles could become a leader in what I have thought of as 'blue diplomacy', based on the presence and potential of the sea as an international resource.

The idea of creole diplomacy (as expressed in the article) is interesting as it reflects what I have always seen as paramount in our dealings with other nations, namely, to bring to the negotiating table a sense of openness which is at the heart of our culture. We would never be compliant for the sake of it but would always negotiate with our partners in pursuit of workable solutions. In acknowledgement of this approach, and out of respect for our integrity, Seychelles was selected in 2014 to chair the Contact Group (CGPCS), the previous holder being the European Union. This was an important sign of trust by the larger nations and it certainly brought kudos to Seychelles 'as an important voice in maritime security affairs'. In the words of my former Foreign Minister:

> *...its openness and its principle of not favouring the interests of one*

partner above another means that despite its small size, Seychelles is able to leverage support for wide-ranging maritime security initiatives.[49]

Small islands on the world stage

I have always admired the writings of the twentieth-century economist, E.F. Schumacher, who in 1973 turned convention on its head in a book with the enduring title, *Small is Beautiful*. Against the trend of making units of government, production and organizations ever-larger, the German-born economist argued that none of this is necessarily of benefit to people, who instinctively prefer things to be smaller and more within reach. Somehow, we need to create a better balance, distinguishing those things, like international bodies, that need to be on a large scale, and those that can better match the level of human access and control. The two dimensions are not necessarily incompatible, so long as the boundaries of each are respected:

> *We always need both freedom and order. We need the freedom of lots and lots of small, autonomous units, and, at the same time, the orderliness of large-scale, possibly global, unity and co-ordination.*[50]

This is how I see Seychelles, enjoying all the virtues of being small but also being able to plug in to the wider, global network of trade and institutions or, in the words of the title of an earlier book of mine, being an *Island Nation in a Global Sea*.[51]

Our geography of scattered islands presents its own communication and governance challenges, though it helps that most of our population is concentrated on three of the inner islands, relatively close to each other. We are also distant from the rest of the world, although by no means remote like we used to be before modern telecommunications, air transport and container shipping. With a small population, there are no economies of scale and the costs of running an effective government are disproportionately high compared with larger states. Our productive land area is very limited and, largely because of this, we have to import most of our goods. If the sea level continues to rise, our coastal plains and even whole islands will be submerged. Our two main economic activities are tourism and fishing, and these will both suffer as a result of the warming of the sea. Like other small island states, our future development, if not our very existence, is under threat.

But Schumacher was right when he extolled the virtues of being small. While never losing sight of the precarious position we are in with the acceleration of climate change, I am also aware that being small has made us what we are. It is not often that a nation can claim, as we do, that we live in a community, with a short but shared history and much in common.

Although we would benefit from more local production, we have at least been spared the ravages (social as well as physical) of destructive industrialization. Our islands remain a source of beauty and pride, our seas largely pristine. Being small bestows qualities that are part of our heritage. In other words, our wish is not to abandon what we value but somehow to integrate that with what we need in order to ensure a sustainable future. Our quest is to find a balance between freedom and order, between the uniqueness of island living and a framework of global order. And this, I believe, is what other small island states are seeking too.

During the years of my presidency, this challenge of integrating small island states within the international community was one that increased in importance. It was there already, before this period, but, as I will show, it had become timely to take the issue onto the world stage. Just as with the case of how we dealt with piracy, creole diplomacy was called for; we had to be smart to be heard. Bringing the agenda of small island states to the attention of the rest of the international community is, inherently, not an easy task, but I always believed it was possible. In the very nature of the undertaking, small islands, individually, have little in the way of power to take to the negotiating table. It worked for us in the case of piracy because many other nations were affected too. But we might not have been so well served had the issue been more localized. So, as a rule, the best chance to provide a platform for small island states to be heard is to work together as a broad-based alliance and to put forward convincing arguments. Especially in the later years of my presidency, once the immediate challenge of the economy had been dealt with, I was able to devote more time to this cause and to work with others to elevate our international standing.

There are, in fact, three international organizations devoted to the interests of small island states and I have been actively involved with each of them. The idea of Small Island Developing States (SIDS) as a distinctive group of countries with their own problems and opportunities dates back to the early 1990s, with the Alliance of Small Island States (AOSIS) the first of the three organizations to be formed.[52] Its main purpose has been to signal the dire effect of global warming on its member states and to play a direct part in international negotiations. It was especially active at the outset in bringing to the world's attention the vulnerability of these nations and is credited for its role in framing the text of the Kyoto Protocol of 1994. I have always acknowledged the importance of AOSIS and its effectiveness in working through its own representatives at the UN headquarters in New York; not only was this an efficient way to operate but it provided direct access to officials and politicians.

The formation of AOSIS was followed in due course by the recognition of small island developing states by the UN in the form of the United Nations Office of the High Representative for the Least Developed Countries, Landlocked Developing Countries and the Small Island Developing States (UN-OHRLLS).[53] Seychelles was a member from the outset yet, while I have always valued the international recognition that comes with this high-sounding but little-known body, there is, unfortunately, a sense that it is designed to serve too many diverse interests. The force for change – and this is no bad thing – would continue to come from the islands themselves, which is why I attached special importance to the third of the three organizations, the Global Island Partnership (GLISPA).

This new body emerged largely as a result of a shared initiative in 2005 by myself and another small island state leader, the President of Palau, Tommy Remengesau. We were both active in the other organizations but saw a gap in their various programmes and priorities, especially in relation to encouraging practical projects. The two of us took a leading role not only in the formation of GLISPA but subsequently in its governance. Membership was, from the outset, diverse (bodies other than nation states were invited to join) and in spite of, or in part because of, its disparate nature it is a more democratic organization than the other bodies working to give a voice to island concerns. There was a strong sense of its leaders speaking for all island people and seeking practical improvements to resist the effects of climate change and other adverse factors. This basic commitment was reflected in the four underlying values, namely: equality, trust, a collaborative approach, and being solution-focused. Continuing priorities bear out the action-based approach of the organization, with a call for all members to launch one new, high-level and visionary sustainable island commitment each year; to accelerate the implementation of sustainable island commitments launched and strengthened through GLISPA; and to 'kick start' one high-impact, demonstration activity in the one of the following: innovative financing for a blue/green economy in islands, sustainable coastal fisheries, and building resilience (ecosystem based adaptation/disaster risk reduction). Additionally, it was with GLISPA's support that I established the Sea Level Rise Foundation (SLRF) in Seychelles as a global initiative to bring together resources and expertise to help small island states, large countries with islands and other low-lying areas to adapt to the growing threat of sea level rise.

My personal interest in representing the interests of small island states was heightened when, in 2011, I saw the need to amplify the message to the United Nations that the idea of sustainability at sea was every bit as important as sustainability on land. I was fortunate that, at the time, the Secretary-General of the UN was Ban Ki-moon, an able and sympathetic diplomat who immediately saw the merits of the case. Small island states, he agreed, deserved an international forum and, with his support, steps were taken that led, in turn, to the designation of 2014 as the International Year of Small Island Developing States. With a high-profile conference held during that year in Samoa, the backing of the UN was indeed a game-changer in asserting the interests of island states like my own. Small Island Developing States (popularly known as SIDS) had something to say which sparked the imagination of many other countries too and Samoa provided the kind of platform we had wished for. To receive this level of recognition so quickly was itself a mark of achievement and a stimulus to further action.

The United Nations is essential to the achievement of international agreements

In speaking up for Seychelles, I enjoyed the support of successive Secretary-Generals of the UN: Kofi Annan and Ban Ki-moon

With such a representative and committed gathering in Samoa, I took every opportunity to press the case that small islands were facing nothing less than an existential crisis. If climate change was to continue unabated, many of these island communities would be lost to rising sea levels. It was a bleak and urgent message but I also raised a banner of hope, calling on the world to acknowledge the potential of a more sustainable use of the oceans. This was a chance for me to explain the importance of the Blue Economy as a concept that we could all support and to argue that small island states could make a unique contribution. People listened and Seychelles was marked firmly on the world map as a source of achievable solutions. Being small was no longer a handicap because the message itself was strong and clear.

In the aftermath of Samoa, there was now a momentum that could no longer be ignored. The outcome of the conference was an action plan named the Samoa Pathway, to which I committed Seychelles, but there was still more to be done. Thus, just two months after Samoa, I convened a meeting in my own country of members of the Alliance of Small Island States so that we could all be better prepared for international negotiations on climate change. In addressing the gathering I shared the view that 'we do not have armies of scientists, statisticians or economists to help us make our case'. But, instead, 'we have something that is invaluable, something that is powerful: we are the conscience of these negotiations. We stand as the defenders of the moral rights of every citizen of our planet'.[54]

I played an active role in the UN event in Samoa, designed to highlight the challenges facing small island states

2014 was, indeed, a pivotal year in bringing the cause of small island states to the attention of the rest of the world. But in a way that was the easy part and, with this level of recognition and support, the real challenge by then was to maintain the momentum. It was time to make things happen and one way to do this was to bring in the business community. As an example of how this could be done, the UN was responsible for the formation of the SIDS Global Business Network:

> *... an online platform and resource hub to share best practices and lessons learned in support of private sector partnerships for small island developing states (SIDS). The network forges collaboration among SIDS regional private sector organizations and works towards strengthening inter-regional business alliances, encouraging international businesses to focus on SIDS as potential market opportunities and vice versa. The SIDS-GBN also fosters greater awareness of the importance of sustainable development as a guide to promoting dynamic business sectors in line with the SAMOA Pathway and the UN's 2030 Agenda for Sustainable Development and Sustainable Development Goals.*[55]

In some ways, Seychelles was already ahead of the game and I would regularly point to an early example of how we had successfully attracted private partners and inward investment to support a new project. This particular venture dates back to 1985, when President René initiated a takeover of the Shell Oil Company's assets in this country and launched a new, publicly-owned, company, the Seychelles Petroleum Company (generally known as SEYPEC). Rather than relying on an overseas enterprise, SEYPEC was designed to take responsibility for importing and distributing the petroleum products on which we are so heavily dependent. In spite of the logic of the plan it was at the time a contentious move, bitterly opposed by the UK because of Shell's British credentials; the new company would undoubtedly be at the expense of the former arrangement. Within Seychelles, there was also some concern that René at first kept the negotiations very much to himself along with an Italian partner, without the involvement of his ministers. Later, it became more transparent and when, in 1989, I was appointed Minister of Finance I saw merit in expanding the project.

Of course, in the interests of sustainable development, my ultimate desire was to see greater use of renewable energy sources based on the wind, tide and sun, and, where possible, we do this in any case. But the relevant technologies are still being perfected and, in the meantime, we rely very largely on imports from the Middle East. I could see that our reliance was not only on the oil itself but also on the foreign-owned tankers. Surely it made better sense, over a period, to buy our own fleet, which could be used for our particular needs but also to trade elsewhere. In the interests of the environment, new vessels could be designed to be as energy-efficient as possible. I took advice from the then CEO of SEYPEC, Captain Guy Adam, who convinced me that the idea was feasible. Thus, through the mechanism of the company, we embarked on the incremental purchase of our own fleet.

Captain Adam had a good understanding of what was available and drew my attention to a German shipyard where production was subsidized by its own government, and prices for their vessels were, as a result, competitive. To add to that, the shipyard could facilitate finance through an associated German bank. The figures added up, on the basis that each new tanker would soon pay for itself and free the way for further purchases. The first off the production line was aptly named 'Seychelles Pride'. Although President René was not initially in favour of the idea, the fleet proved to be a highly successful enterprise and trading profits were ploughed back to repay loans. Once the debts arising from the purchase of the tankers were settled, the arrangement yielded obvious financial benefits for the country. But there are other advantages too, including a source of local employment and the development of a skilled labour force, and also control over the quality of imports to meet higher environmental standards.

This, of course, is only one example but it illustrates how home-born ideas can be of value, not only to the country of origin but as a model for other small nations too. As I will explain in a later chapter, I remain active in promoting business enterprise as an essential activity for small island states.

Making the New Seychelles Work

The world as we have created it, is a product of our thinking. It cannot be changed without changing our thinking.[56]

Whether, as Albert Einstein conjectured, the world cannot be changed without changing our thinking is, in a literal sense, a moot point as it certainly cannot be achieved without action as well. But it is undoubtedly true that the world around us is a product, at least in part, of the way we interpret it. In my own situation, unprecedented changes were made in Seychelles following the introduction in 1977 of the Second Constitution and, in spite of the advent, after 1993, of multi-party politics, we followed a well-trodden path for the rest of that century. Indeed, even when I became president in 2004, the political landscape had not changed that much. Our thinking was deeply rooted in what had become so familiar, the product of a socialist ideology which put its trust in the state to achieve a fair and just society. As a leading figure in government for all those years I had myself become immersed in that way of thinking. But I could also see that the world was changing and not all aspects of the previous system were working as they should. Of course, I maintained my belief in the goal of a fair and just society but I had grown increasingly sceptical about the ultimate power of the state to deliver this. In other words, if I thought there was a better way of doing things, I was open to new ideas.

Firm but fair

By the time I won my own mandate in 2006, my thinking had already evolved and it was with confidence that I spoke increasingly about the 'New Seychelles'. It was a term that neatly summed up my attempt to chart a fresh course for the nation and the outcome was to mark another important element of my legacy. Without delay, my government set its sights on new horizons and we shared our thoughts with the people. If this break with the past was to work, it was not just the thinking of a few that had to change but the thinking of all – and I had no illusions about the immensity of the task. Rather like turning a giant ocean tanker, it would necessarily be a slow and measured process. We could not afford to lose the momentum built up over the years but I was convinced that, for the benefit of the nation, it had become necessary to alter the direction of the ship of state.

Some things that had been right in the past had by then lost their lustre. The state had brought about much-needed change but it seemed that inertia had since set in; strong leadership had enabled far-reaching reforms, but that approach had now to be balanced by a more robust form of democracy; private enterprise had been poorly regarded in the socialist era but no longer could this be the case; deficit budgets had become the norm but, in the face of imminent bankruptcy, there was an urgent need to change that. The world did not owe us a living and in future we had to pay our way. All of which touched on every aspect of our lives. The New Seychelles could not be bought cheaply but the potential gains for the whole nation were enormous. It is this approach which would mark my presidency.

This was not an easy message to get across but, step by step and with the support of my ministers, I took every opportunity to urge the nation forward in this new direction. It was important to recognize how far we had come since independence but also that there were fresh challenges to confront. I could rightly claim that over the years the ruling party had changed the whole order of things, replacing a bitterly divided society with one that had become more equal and where new opportunities for all had been created. But there was still further to go and I used one of my annual addresses to the nation to paint a picture of where that might lead:

> *A prosperous nation that is intelligent, united and harmonious. A society that is caring and compassionate. A responsible government leading to a force of workers who are disciplined, motivated and serious, and also responsible citizens who are ready to take responsibility for their own future. A country that empowers its citizens, that provides them with adequate resources and the tools to enable them to earn a living, and to create wealth. A country that has zero tolerance for corruption, criminality and social delinquency. A country that is actively encouraging innovation and creativity. We can all see ourselves in the New Seychelles.*[57]

From my perspective as president, the key to making the New Seychelles a reality was to ensure good governance and to improve the workings of democracy. These two elements would go hand in hand. For a start, every nation which seeks to improve the lot of its people is dependent on good governance. It has to be all-embracing to include the public and private sectors, central as well as local government, non-governmental as well as government organizations. Like a well-oiled machine it has to be maintained and not distorted by negative forces like corruption. Indeed, from the outset, I declared that I would outlaw corruption as it is just another term for stealing money from the people.

From time to time, political opponents would make false accusations about corruption involving one person or another and (as I explain in a later chapter) I always took the opportunity to put the facts straight. I am a great believer in transparency, which is itself an essential ingredient of democracy. Had we not been entirely open about our economic reforms I am convinced that we would not have won the popular support that we did. There was a cost for all Seychellois but being entirely honest about the process and outcomes was at the heart of the decision that we should go ahead. No-one likes to swallow bitter medicine unless, that is, one can be sure that it will lead to better health. In the event, we took the medicine and were, before too long, better as a result.

Nor was corruption confined to domestic issues and one of the biggest challenges I faced was the fact that Seychelles had an unwanted reputation in the international community as a place where illegal activities flourished. This had to stop. As I explain in the following section, I placed a high priority on introducing new measures to bring propriety and dignity to all of our dealings. We were no longer a one-party state but had yet to live up to all of the noble ideas of the Third Republic (dating from the country's return to multi-party politics) in which the constitution pledges recognition of 'the inherent dignity and the equal and inalienable rights of all members of the human family as the foundation for freedom, justice, welfare, fraternity, peace and unity'.

Meeting international standards

Ironically, in the interests of good governance, the actions that had to be taken needed to be handled with a degree of discretion. For all my commitment to transparency, there were some things that could only be put in place behind the scenes. In particular, soon after taking up my presidential post, I saw the need to urgently address the fact that the country was without a properly organized and professional system to collect and act upon intelligence; we were rather like a ship heading out to sea without navigational aids, reliant solely on the captain's orders. This is how it had been during the period of one-party rule and nothing seemed to have changed since then. Urgent action was needed because, in different ways, not only was the country's security at risk but also our very reputation in the international community. We would never win the respect of nations unless we could first manage, in a principled way, our own territory.

I have already spoken of the need to combat piracy and, with the help of international partners, our intelligence in this sector gradually improved. We became more effective at sea and were responsible for some outstanding anti-piracy actions; in turn, we duly passed a new law so that we could prosecute captured pirates in Seychelles. In this way we became the hub for the judicial treatment of Somali pirates in the region and a primary player in international operations. No-one should underestimate the significance of taking this kind of lead as it carried with it the threat of retaliatory action by dissident forces in Somalia, whose interests and criminal activities were clearly threatened. But it was time to show, unequivocally, where Seychelles stood on the issue of piracy and not to be deterred by the threat of potential retaliation.

While some progress was made on that front, in other respects things were getting worse. We were attracting an unwanted reputation as a small island state where money laundering could flourish. With a miniscule population in relation to the rest of the world we accommodated in the region of 15% of the global total of offshore companies, many of which were simply facilitating the illegal movement of capital. Especially in the aftermath of the break-up of the Soviet Union and the control of state assets by mafia-type organizations, together with an upsurge in the international drugs trade, there was no shortage of dirty money in search of a safe hiding place. It was clear that Seychelles was being used as one such venue and this was seriously affecting our reputation as an open and honest society.

I was also only too aware of the inflow of increasing quantities of heroin, which could only happen with the connivance of some individuals within our own agencies. This was a matter of special concern to me, not simply because the laws of the country were being flouted but because it was a human tragedy, destroying the lives of too many young (and not so young) people. Beyond these specific instances, the presence of particular criminal activities attracts other ones too; organized crime gains a foothold and before long it is not only money laundering and drugs but also the threat of people trafficking, contraband in the form of tobacco and alcohol, and the banned movement of endangered species. To add to it all, criminals were often keen to buy a property in Seychelles from where they could base their activities.

This situation had to be countered before the rot set in too far. For me, there was only one way to do so, namely, through rooting out culpable individuals and putting in place accountable institutions. A government cannot work effectively without reliable information nor can it operate on the basis of individual informers and hearsay; robust institutions have to be in place. In many ways, the problems confronting us were inter-related: our intelligence was weak, little was being done to prevent drugs entering the country, and there were huge inflows of tainted money. As a result, I took advice on how other countries were dealing with these same problems.

Money laundering was an obvious starting point and as soon as possible I ensured that new legislation was passed, a feature of which was the creation of a dedicated Financial Intelligence Unit. With this in place, we now had the power to confiscate illegally-acquired assets and transfer them to the Treasury, and before long there were many instances where this was done. Between 2009 and 2016 some 450 million rupees were intercepted and in the last year when I was in office, no less than 110 million rupees were transferred to the state in this way. Moreover, from being effectively blacklisted, the international view by then was that Seychelles was performing well above the accepted norm.

I also introduced new anti-drugs legislation and created the National Drugs Enforcement Agency, which acted independently of the police (where there was clear evidence of connivance with the smugglers). In the period that followed, large quantities of heroin were seized, and drug-traffickers prosecuted. Shortly before I stepped down in 2016, for instance, the NDEA intercepted an Iranian dhow in our maritime space, carrying no less than 96 kg of heroin. It was a successful strategy which reduced the inflow of drugs and pushed the outer limits of illegal activities further from our shores.

For the sake of our national security, I was also determined that there should be an institutional response. While some of the immediate issues could be contained through the FIU, with the help of consultants we prepared the architecture for a national intelligence system (NIS). Everything was ready for approval by the Cabinet and National Assembly, only to be delayed by the onset of elections.

I regard the work I did in these spheres as an important part of my legacy, getting to grips at last with a rotten core of illegal activities. I was well aware of criminal interests opposed to my actions but I was determined to drive through the changes and to set Seychelles on a new path, so that we could hold our heads high in the international community.

The legacy takes shape

Five years into my presidency, I was asked what I had achieved and where the nation was heading:

> *Well, the five years which have passed have allowed me to lay the foundations, to create the tools which are necessary for us as a people to get up, walk tall and work, to continue to develop our country and bring it forward. To me this is a beginning. To me now is the hour to start work. I am sure that when the two years ahead of us [before the next presidential election] will have passed, I will have consolidated a modern economy for Seychelles. I will face the electorate, the Seychellois people, and ask them to judge me by my actions, my work to bring our country where we are today, a country with a better governance, more transparency, better conditions in*

our democracy to create a modern economy to bring a better life for Seychellois.[58]

In other words, I knew then that we were on course in our journey to make the New Seychelles. The next presidential election came two years later and I was returned with a convincing majority to continue along this path. Five years after that, I passed yet another test, winning my third such election. I then chose during my fourth term to stand down, having led the country for twelve years; but I did so knowing that I could pass on a priceless legacy – the legacy of a successful nation. Nor was that my view alone and I could refer for hard evidence to various independent sources; the nation was, indeed, doing well.[59] The New Seychelles was already a reality.

- From being an impoverished group of islands far from the mainland of Africa, during my presidency Seychelles was categorized by the World Bank as one of the world's high-income countries.

- We also fared well on the UN's Human Development Index, coming first amongst all of the African countries.

- Foreign investment was at last flowing into the country at a sufficient rate to maintain our global activities; by the time I left office, the foreign exchange reserve in the Central Bank was more than half a billion US dollars.

- The nation had gained the respect of the international community for its measures to turn back the global tide of criminal activities; we were winning the battle against organized crime.

- A strong institutional framework was in place, facilitating good governance in all spheres of activity.

- In one of my last acts as president I changed the constitution to restrict the terms of future presidencies to two mandates. When the Secretary-General of the UN visited Seychelles soon after, he said that this was an example of exemplary democracy for the whole of Africa.

- Important foreign debts were written off in favour of spending on our marine environment, a vital stimulus for our Blue Economy plans.

- The target of protecting 30% of the sea within our jurisdiction won praise from leading campaigners for ocean sustainability and is seen as a model for others to emulate.

- On our islands, 50% of the land area is now protected and I was responsible for launching our National Biodiversity Centre.

- Helped by the buoyancy of our tourist industry (more than a quarter of a million visitors arrived in 2015), rates of unemployment were consistently low.

- With 94% of the population literate (99% for young people), this is the envy of most of our African neighbours.

- Every young person, regardless of family income, enjoys free access to education up to at least the fifth year of secondary school and those who can progress beyond that are eligible for technical education and university attendance too; Seychelles was the first African country to achieve this level of support for young people.

- Communicable diseases have been largely eradicated and health standards are constantly improving; year on year, people are living longer: the average life expectancy in 2015 was 74.2 years.

- The youth of the country was well served, with innovative schemes like a national university and a project to equip young leaders for their future roles.

- The plight of less fortunate members of society was addressed through a national renaissance initiative.

- 93% of households were connected to a treated water supply while others choose to rely on fresh water from the mountains.

- Electricity was supplied to 97% of all households.

- With foreign exchange more freely available in the country, businesses flourished and people could at last buy what had previously been denied to them.

- Amongst the most obvious purchases was the private car, with possession by roughly half of all households, but other consumer products were much prized too.

- Elections are held regularly and win the approval of independent observers.

One of the treasured aspects of my legacy: the annual Graduation Day at UniSey

Of course, there was no room for complacency and there is always room for improvement. I would be the first to admit that everything was not perfect. We had come a long way but there was further to go. The fact is that society was changing fast and, with the emergence of a strong middle class, it was vital to ensure that the poorest in society were not left behind. I saw this as something that my successor would need to address. The New Seychelles depends on keeping the situation under constant review and on a willingness to adopt new policies.

In looking ahead, I never forgot the contribution of the elderly to making Seychelles the country it is now

With the support of the UAE, we were able to make a valuable start in harnessing wind energy

There was much, though, to build on. Ours was already a mixed economy with a global reach; our people are well educated and committed to the transition of Seychelles to a knowledge economy; our democracy can be a model of its kind, extending to all levels of society. We were well on the way to fulfilling this vision. When I stood down in 2016, I could hold my head high; I knew that I had done everything I could to make this possible. It was with a sense of pride that I handed the keys of my office to my successor.

Such is my legacy.

Part 2

Through a Glass, Darkly

*For now we see through a glass, darkly; but then face to face:
Now I know in part; but then shall I know even as also I am known...*[60]

- ❖ **Succession**
- ❖ **Shadows**
- ❖ **Identity**
- ❖ **Reflection**

Succession

And a new people takes the land: and still it is not we.[61]

National elections in Seychelles take place in two stages, the first being presidential and the second on a district basis to elect members to the National Assembly. Each presidential election normally occurs on a five-year cycle and it is the prerogative of the newly incumbent president to propose a date for the second stage of the process.

During my second term of office, I had to decide whether to stand again in 2015. The constitution at the time allowed me to do so for one more term. In this chapter I share my reasons for coming to the decision to stand for re-election and I give my view of the various outcomes that followed, leading in the following year to the transfer of power and inauguration of a new president.

The elections which duly took place in 2015 and 2016 redrew an important part of the political landscape. In the presidential election in 2015, I was returned with a very narrow majority. But in the following year, when the electorate voted for local representatives, the balance of power in the National Assembly swung in favour of the opposition parties. As such, it proved to be a testing time for our young nation, although our democratic system and the resilience of the people both proved to be sufficiently robust to withstand the challenge. This is something in which we should all take pride. There are not so many countries in the region which would have been able to achieve this and I pay tribute to the commitment of opposition politicians to make it work, as well as members of my own party.

In successive elections, our democratic system has proved robust, with high turnouts and peaceful acceptance of outcomes

One year into my new term of office, I decided to hand over the presidency to my successor. For me, personally, it marked a decisive break from my life on the frontline of politics. It was a time of mixed emotions but one advantage was that, as the dust settled, I could see more clearly just how much was changing around me. With the benefit of hindsight, I can now reflect on the transition process and the new political landscape that emerged.

Remaining at the Helm

I am the captain of my soul.[62]

When Nelson Mandela affirmed that he was captain of his soul there would have been few people to disagree. Mandela was a brave leader whose integrity was surely beyond question. It is unlikely that he could have ventured into such contentious territory without firmly believing that his actions were in step with his inner beliefs. Big decisions require this strong sense of conviction.

Well before the 2015 election I gave serious thought to whether I should stand again. It was a time to question my own beliefs as well as to balance these with national considerations. The eventual decision was not taken lightly and it was certainly not an automatic reaction dictated by election dates. Perhaps it was because I had a sixth sense that change was in the offing that I took my own time to carefully weigh up the various pros and cons.

On the one hand, there were strong reasons for re-standing. By then I had been president for the best part of a decade and my appetite to lead the country was undiminished. Seychelles was faring well and I knew that I had already created a valuable legacy. My advisers confirmed that there was a high level of satisfaction with my leadership and the government's policies. In the middle of my mandate resulting from the previous elections, forecasts for the next presidential contest were not anticipating an upset and I was advised that I should be returned to office in 2015 with at least 55% of the vote. The signs were undoubtedly favourable and I was certainly tempted to stand again. And yet, in spite of the positive predictions, I felt an inner twinge of unease. With change in the air, perhaps the situation was not quite as straightforward as first appeared.

Being an oceanic state, we are fond of metaphors which reflect our maritime setting and, in this respect, it was as if I were at the helm of a ship sailing smoothly across the sea, confident that we were on course to reach our destination. But, as an experienced mariner, something was also telling me that beneath the surface there were flows tugging in a different direction. Undercurrents are, by their very nature, not easy to track but, equally, they will reveal themselves sooner or later. I had a very real sense that the sea might yet have surprises in store.

Sometimes, when confronting a difficult situation, it is good to remove oneself from familiar surroundings and day-to-day pressures, to reflect quietly on where to go next. And so it was that an opportunity arose when I attended an international conference in Yokohama, Japan, with time one afternoon to step aside and give thought to the decision that, before too long, I would have to confirm. I weighed up the arguments and kept coming back to one factor that gave me particular concern, namely, whether I could be confident that my successor would, by the time of the next election, be sufficiently experienced to take over and lead Parti Lepep to another victory. After careful thought, I concluded that it was too soon to hand over.

Danny Faure had already shown himself to be a competent vice-president and was the obvious contender for the top post. What is more, he would be able to call on very talented individuals in the wings to join his team, such as Jean-Paul Adam; but I was not convinced that Danny himself was quite ready at that stage to lead the party into a presidential election. With more experience I was sure he had the potential to become a good leader, but not just yet. If he failed to win the next election, I was concerned about the effects this would have on the country. This was not a time to gamble; there was just too much to lose. And so, from faraway Japan, I returned to Seychelles with my mind clear on the subject. I would stand once again for the presidency. There would be time enough then to hand over to my successor, in time for him to prepare his own mandate for 2020.

Continuity is a political asset and I was always heartened by the fact that I was leading the party with the most consistent record in Seychelles. For nearly four decades before the upcoming presidential election in 2015, the political party which I have always supported had remained in power. Details of our programmes changed over the years but our priorities throughout this period were unwavering. We assumed power in 1977 with the goal of creating a fairer society that would bring benefits to all Seychellois – and when it came to presenting my manifesto in 2015, this was still our goal. The consistency of our stance is why I believe I was again returned to office, just as my predecessor and I had won previous elections on this same platform.

Of course, nothing is forever and radical policies such as ours were always going to attract opposition as well as support. From the outset, there were many in the privileged class who resisted a shift in the balance of power and wealth away from their own interests. Some left the country at the time of the regime change in 1977, but others tried to adapt to the new ways, perhaps hoping that the pendulum would swing back in their favour if they were patient. Meanwhile, it is a fact of political life that people in a democracy will often opt for change, if only because they think it is in itself due; it is frequently said that 'it is time for a change', as if that, on its own, is a good enough reason to do so. Politicians themselves will often see the pendulum of popular opinion swinging against them as if it is inevitable. But they are wrong to do so and the truth is that the electorate can see what they too easily miss, namely, that complacency is corrosive and the people are being taken for granted.

Throughout my career as a politician, I have always kept close to the people I serve. That has not been a calculating move, simply to secure more votes, but I have done this because I understand and share their concerns. I have never forgotten my own background, shaped by poverty, and it is this experience which has nurtured my own aspirations to help those in a similar situation. Sadly, though, I have witnessed the fact that too many of the new generations of politicians have neglected the people, preferring to spend their time in committees and overseas trips. They have sometimes secured jobs for their friends and relatives, at the expense of hardworking contenders. I have constantly tried to demonstrate that their approach is not acceptable but they are content to do things their way. Little wonder that the essential bond between politicians and the people has too often become frayed. At some stage, I could see that it would, inevitably, snap.

And so it was that, although the political opposition had not been especially effective over the years, time was on their side and I knew that things would be closer in the coming election than they had been in the past. Indeed, while, as a result of the popular vote, I was duly returned to office, I was correct in my belief that the wider political landscape was changing. For me, and for my country, a new era was about to begin; we were together entering uncharted territory.

The Will of the People

For us democracy is a question of human dignity. And human dignity is political freedom.[63]

The above quote by the former Prime Minister of Sweden, Olof Palme, resonates with my own beliefs. Human dignity is at the heart of civilized politics and, whatever our differences, unless we continue to treat each other with respect then political freedom itself will be in jeopardy. A changing political landscape is not in itself necessarily injurious but if it brings with it disrespect for the views of the people, it threatens the very essence of democracy. In the face of new alignments in party politics in Seychelles, it is a credit to the country that the institution of democracy stood firm – even though (as will be shown later) there were a few participants who, sadly, were prepared to abandon some of the key values that we had all supported over the years.

Although the 2015 presidential election was to be held in September of that year it was delayed until December to allow all parties to make sufficient preparations. Apart from the two-month delay, the election proceeded in the usual way, spread, as always, over three days because of the dispersed geography of the country. This time there were six candidates (myself included) in contention. A variety of posters quickly adorned the roadsides and there was great interest in the contest to come. The election duly took place and when the result was announced it was clear that I had come out well ahead of any of the other candidates, recording a personal vote of 28,911 compared with 21,391 for the next in line, Wavel Ramkalawan. Especially given the very high turnout (87.4%), this was a solid endorsement from the people of Seychelles. However, in spite of this convincing outcome, because of the number of votes won by other parties, my majority was not quite enough to reach the threshold of 50% required to ensure outright victory. As a result, for the first time in the history of Seychelles, a second presidential election was held two weeks later.

On the basis of the figures in the first round, the challenge of gaining sufficient votes at the next stage to cross the 50% threshold was formidable; in effect, I had to attract an additional 3000 votes and I had only two weeks to do so. Given the very high turnout in the first election it was unlikely that this extra number could be drawn wholly from people who had chosen not to vote then. Instead, it was apparent that I would need to persuade active voters to switch their allegiance in favour of my own candidacy. There was hardly sufficient time to convince this number in the short period before the second election but our party supporters rallied to the cause and everyone worked through all hours to press home the case. In the event, it was a highly successful campaign and once again I received the largest vote, only this time I also exceeded the required 50% majority. In itself, it was, indeed, a cause for celebration. There was, however, a sting in the tail. Compared with the first round, the margin of victory was very much narrower. The reason for this is easy to see. Patrick Pillay, the candidate who had come third in the original election with 8,593 votes, along with two more contestants from the first round, weighed in this time to support Wavel Ramkalawan, and it was concluded that this move was instrumental in closing the gap between the other parties and myself to just 193 votes.

As participants in the democratic process, we could all share a sense of pride. There had been enormous interest in the contest and more than 90% of the electorate cast their vote, a proportion that very few democracies are able to achieve. Another sign of the strength of our respect for democracy was that the outcome was accepted in a peaceful manner; some people feared there would be protests on the streets but that was not the case. It is to the credit of all political parties and, not least of all, to the maturity of the electorate, that there were no attempts to overturn the result. Thus, with 50.15% of the votes cast in my favour, I was able to begin a new term as president.

In spite of the intense interest in the election, and the prospect of parliamentary elections to come, there was no time to be lost in getting on with running the country; 'business as usual' was uppermost in our minds. Indeed, in the circumstances, the need to demonstrate the confidence and energy of the government was even more important than usual. As a result, I took every opportunity to pass on the message that we were intent on continuing the good work of my previous administrations and we began the task without delay. In my inauguration speech, I immediately announced an ambitious programme for the first 100 days, and my ministers, in their respective areas, were held to account to deliver on our promises. Improving service delivery especially in the public sector, job creation, empowerment of the private sector, improving access to credit for people wanting to have their own home, as well as the fight against drugs, were some of the priorities highlighted. In order to stop drugs entering the country, I could see (rather like the case of piracy) that we would be unable to solve this problem on our own and would, instead, need the support of neighbouring countries. That is why I proposed the setting up of a new regional structure for intelligence, coordination and operations to combat drug trafficking at the level of the existing regional body, the Indian Ocean Commission.

My third presidential inauguration ceremony, in 2015, was another historic occasion to mark my political career

Then, in February, came my annual State of the Nation Address and with that the chance to provide a more detailed programme for the coming term. I laid great emphasis on what could be done to support people in greatest need. Housing would continue to be a priority and I looked forward to the day when every Seychellois family could live in their own home, rather than have to share or experience sub-standard conditions. There were still disparities in income between different groups and it was the task of government to reduce these to give everyone a fair chance of improvement. Great progress had been made over the years in education and health provision but I was critical of those who were responsible for delivering services that failed to meet our expected standards. Poor performance could not be tolerated in the public sector, any more than it would be allowed by shareholders in private businesses. Everyone needed to pull together.

At the same time, I would have been remiss to have ignored the rifts that had opened up in the course of the recent elections. There was a noticeable change in the political environment. False accusations were made at the time of campaigning and promises made by opposition parties that could never be delivered. I urged that we should put that episode behind us and recognize once again that we have more to bring us together than to divide us. My annual address ended with an assurance that 'this Parti Lepep government will continue to work for all Seychellois. For our wellbeing, our prosperity and the progress of our country'. And I reminded the people that we would shortly be celebrating the 40th anniversary of our independence:

> *If we have reached where we are today, it is thanks to our determination and our conviction that, within us Seychellois, we have the courage to stand up and do what is right for our Seychelles. We have done it TOGETHER. Now my call as the President of Seychelles is for us all to rally together to consolidate our unity, to preserve our stability and to continue to make the Seychelles that we love remain that country of peace and unity in the world.*[64]

As the year unfolded, I worked hard with my ministers to deliver on all of our pledges. We had a very full agenda and it was not until September 2016 that, as the constitution allows, we called the parliamentary elections. The four main opposition parties combined to form a coalition, Linyon Demokratik Seselwa (LDS); and another opposition party, the Seychelles Patriotic Movement, fought the election under its own banner. Three independent candidates also stood in their own constituencies. In effect, this amounted to a case of Parti Lepep versus the rest, although the heart of the contest was between my own party and the coalition. Given how close the outcome was in the presidential election, we knew that this would inevitably be a keen contest. As a result, we all campaigned hard once again and on election day it was soon apparent that there would be another high turnout (87.5% on this occasion).

The aggregate vote was every bit as close as we expected (a majority of just 216 in favour of the LDS) but, because of the disposition of constituencies, the allocation of seats in the National Assembly resulted in 19 for the LDS and 14 for Parti Lepep. Additionally, according to the rules, another four seats went to each side on the basis of proportional representation. Wavel Ramkalawan failed to win a constituency seat in the open election but entered the National Assembly through one of the PR seats due to his party; he subsequently assumed the position of Leader of the Opposition.

The people of Seychelles had spoken and the outcome was a binary form of government. It all looked very different from what had evolved over the previous decades. The balance of power had been transformed. A multi-party democracy was now a reality. I had already been elected as president but now a majority of seats in the National Assembly was occupied by opposition representatives. An unprecedented constitutional situation had been created but I was confident that this could be handled fairly, in the best interests of the country. We had faced challenges before and emerged with dignity; we could do this now too.

Transfer of Power

In one of the most inspiring speeches made in Africa in recent times, Michel said power was not an aim in itself but a means to do good for the people... the interests of the nation come first.[65]

Our democratic structure was once again tested, and once again it proved more than equal to the challenge. There was a smooth transition, first in the presidential election when my majority was so slim and now in the parliamentary follow-up, which resulted in a radical shift in power in the National Assembly. Little wonder that observers of African elections (as the above quote demonstrates) commended our country for its handling of democracy. It was, in all respects, exemplary.

Certainly, my position as president had changed. But I had no doubt that I could adapt to that. I would still chair my Cabinet of Ministers and be the voice of Seychelles in international relations. Unlike in the past I would not have as much room to manoeuvre and the National Assembly would exercise its own powers to the full; in its way, of course, I saw that this could enhance the workings of democracy. It was an unprecedented situation for Seychelles but, in fact, it is how many (if not most) other democratic systems operate. The constitution of the United States, for instance, is built around a series of checks and balances and it is not unusual for the House of Representatives and the Senate each to be in the hands of a different political majority. Even more widespread is the evidence of coalitions, elected through proportional representation rather than a simple majority vote, where the elected leader has constantly to bear in mind the interests of all parties. In many ways, our own situation seemed simpler to handle and I was fully prepared to accept the challenge. Yet, it was also timely to take stock of the new situation and assess its wider impact.

By September 2016 I had been in office for more than twelve years (since

April 2004) and, while there is always more to do, I believed that the country was in good shape. Nearly a year had passed since I was returned to office and, not only had I used that time to reaffirm the way ahead, but my vice-president had gained more experience in the process. Assuming the next presidential election would be in 2020, I could choose to remain until then, but not beyond that. The introduction of my recent measure, to limit presidential terms to no more than two, meant that I could not stand for election again. In fact, I had always thought that it would be sensible to hand over to my successor before then, to enable that person to become familiar with the workings of high office before standing for election in their own right. That was how I had been inducted myself in 2004, and I found the period of overlap extremely helpful as an individual. Of greater importance, this seemed to work well for the country as it was entirely constitutional and would offer the least disruption to the business of government. The only question for me was to decide when this handover should be.

On balance, I had originally thought that it would take place after one further year of my new term. But I had to bear in mind the effects on the incoming president of the constitutional change I had recently introduced, which would limit the number of elections to be contested to two. Danny Faure was vice-president and, assuming he subsequently won his elections, the longest he could serve as president would be the two five-year periods between elections plus however long before 2020. In my view, if I were to stand down late in 2016, he was young enough to lead the country for the full term. Having successfully negotiated his way through two recent elections, he had proved himself to be experienced and we had worked well together in our respective posts. So that is what I did, announcing at the start of October 2016 that I would, forthwith, transfer the presidency to my vice-president. My right to do so was entirely within the jurisdiction – and the spirit – of the constitution and, contrary to the objections of the opposition, there were no grounds to call another election.

When I did this, some people believed that the real reason was because I was not prepared to confront the new political situation, confronting an opposition majority in the National Assembly. As I have explained above, that was certainly not the case. I was fully prepared to do so had the need arisen, but I was by then convinced that it would be in the best interests of the country if I were to stand down without needless delay. In any case, having been responsible for changing the constitution to limit the terms of office for future presidents, I could hardly justify staying in office for more that twelve years. Moreover, apart from any other reasons, with an early transfer of power, the new president would be able to forge from the outset his own relationship with the opposition and ensure that the government of the country operated effectively.

I spoke to Danny Faure and he expressed his readiness, as well as great enthusiasm, to take over. There were protocols to observe and an inauguration ceremony was organized to appoint the country's fourth president. On 16 October 2016, guests gathered on the lawn in front of State House and the formal handover took place. Warm words were spoken and it all boded well. In my own address, I said that I had done things 'my way', which was a cue for my talented protocol officer, Gervais Moumou, to offer a rendition of the song of that title in 'his way'. I then went on to conclude that:

> *After all these years spent as a minister and vice-president and the 12 years spent as president, I felt the time had come for me to hand over the presidency to a younger leader who would pursue the work we started more than 52 years ago. I am sure Mr Danny Faure will do a good job as president. Danny, please take good care of this country, stay humble, stay connected with the people. I can assure you of all my support and wish you all the best as President of Seychelles and I call on all Seychellois to do the same.*

I recalled that I had by then spent more than 2,500 weeks in politics, when many believe that one week in that arena can be a lifetime in itself. Yet I had never tired of the experience, and my enthusiasm to serve my country was undiminished.

In his response, the new president acknowledged the debt he owed to me, saying that during the course of our journey filled with many challenges he had learned to always keep his sights focused on the issues greater than ourselves: that is, the welfare of the people of our country:

> *Today, after you have completed 39 years in the Cabinet of Ministers, including 12 years as president, I salute you for your personal sacrifice, your hard work and your dedication in the service of the people of Seychelles. I join the entire Seychellois nation in wishing you all the very best in your retirement, and to accord you the respect that you deserve.*[66]

He added that, under my presidency, Seychelles had witnessed an unprecedented economic transformation.

On the following day, protocol was again observed when, together with the founding president, Sir James Mancham, I returned to State House for a customary tea with the new president. There was a proper sense of dignity and respect about it, part of the formal ritual of the handover. But, as events were soon to show, it was not to last. Certainly, I had not intended to interfere in the work of my successor but I was surprised that my name so quickly slipped down the official protocol list. I was not invited to future events of national importance, nor even to informal meetings with the new president to share ideas and experience. Visiting heads of state came and went, and (even though I sometimes knew the distinguished visitors) I was regularly excluded from receptions. When the new president spoke in his inauguration speech of my retirement, I was soon to see that he used the word in a literal sense. In his eyes I was already yesterday's man. The disappointment for me was not so much personal but rather because I knew there was still so much more I could have done to help my country.

For all our political differences, the founding president and I developed a healthy respect and even friendship for each other

Perhaps I should not have been so surprised by the immediacy of the change. As Sir James remarked to me at the time, he had many so-called friends when he was president but these quickly disappeared when he was deposed. In any case, President Faure had his own agenda and he would, understandably, want to make an early start with his new programme. If it came as a shock that he did not want to share his ideas, I suppose it was in part because I was thinking of how I had earlier responded to my own predecessors. I had worked closely over a long period with the former president, France Albert René, and when I succeeded him, we would at first meet on a regular basis to discuss issues. We both belonged to the same political party but our association was about more than that. In the same way, although the founding president, James Mancham, came from a very different social and political background, I accorded him the respect of asking him, on occasions, to represent me at high-profile, overseas events. We held opposing political views but were united by our love of Seychelles and a common desire to serve our country; indeed, with so much in common, we developed a friendship that went beyond party boundaries.

So, as with my own predecessors, when I was succeeded as president, I thought I might still have a role to play, not in any direct sense of being part of government but rather as a loyal citizen and friend. One area where I had gained international recognition was in the promotion of the Blue Economy and I would have been more than prepared to have acted in an ambassadorial role, spreading the message for Seychelles and bringing home the lessons gained from other countries. But that was not to be and, instead, I found myself, still full of energy and ideas, not to mention experience and contacts, now effectively excluded from events, and sidelined in other ways too.

At no time, in official circles, was my past contribution to the development of Seychelles formally acknowledged. Even at an informal level, ministers who I had so recently worked with revealed to me that they had been strongly warned against continuing to meet me and that they should not even mention my name. One senior minister suggested to the new president that I could still have a role to play with the Blue Economy, but this was summarily dismissed. It was clear that President Faure saw this now as his domain, no doubt as a means to gain credibility in the international community. Not only was I excluded from ministerial circles but also I discovered that my previously strong links within Parti Lepep had been noticeably weakened, and the veto on referring to me by name was even extended to party representatives in the National Assembly. The break with the past was total. It was if the ascendancy of Danny Faure marked Year Zero; history had been erased.

In the following chapter I will try to get to grips with why this was the case. Why did people I had worked with so closely over the years turn so suddenly against me? What was it that motivated people, many of whom I had never met, to write so vehemently on social media? And, of greatest concern, what effects was this having on the country I love? Shadows were spreading across the islands where so recently it seemed the sun would always shine. I was losing sight of the Seychelles I knew, and it was this which grieved me most of all.

Danny Faure and I worked well together when I was still president but when he took over he looked in a different direction

Shadows

Shadows: beyond the reach of the sun, the dark side of the moon.[67]

Shadows are not a mere figment of the imagination. They cannot be touched but they are real. Not only real but transformative, casting in their subtle way all that is familiar, literally, into a different light. Rather like an eclipse of the sun, the brightness of the earth can be shrouded in gloom in a matter of minutes. It is disconcerting at the time but it soon passes, and it is this certainty which encourages me to look more closely at the process. In doing so, let me call once again on William Shakespeare, who in one of his sonnets, asked this probing question:

> *What is your substance, whereof you are made,*
> *That millions of strange shadows on you tend?*

What, indeed, is the substance? And why the shadows?

Dark Corners of the Universe

The universe has a dark corner, the human soul, which is its reflection.[68]

No matter how benign one is about humanity, there are dark corners of the universe where one's faith is challenged. It would be all too easy to explain this in terms of 'good people' and 'bad people' but that is not what I believe. There is good and bad in profusion, yet life offers us all, whatever our disposition, a chance to breathe – though sometimes it is true that circumstances tilt the balance, in favour of one or the other.

In this respect, political circumstances can be especially pervasive. I am only too aware that politics and the quest for power can be a potent mix that some find hard to resist; and in pursuit of advancement, lines of trust are too easily crossed. How many political leaders and dynasties from around the world can one cite to make the point? Almost on a weekly basis there are reports of so-called democratic elections questioned by the people. How many individuals, in a position of power, then proceed to act as if they have been blessed to walk on water? Examples of the latter include not only the obvious cases of dictatorships but also advanced democracies where charges of corruption regularly destroy reputations and bring down governments. Ultimately, it is likely that transgressors will be taken to task, but a tendency to bestow too much power on too few people remains an unfortunate weakness in many political systems. Fortunately, Seychelles fares better in international indicators of good governance than many other nations. But the temptation created by the system is always there and to avoid the misuse of power, shrewd judgement at the highest level, as well as sound values, is essential. In building my own legacy this is something that I have always sought, not only in my own actions but from those around me too.

With hindsight, in trying to explain why some people turned against me after I stepped down as president, my view is that it had its origins amongst a small but powerful group of individuals who were almost certainly conspiring well before 2016. It was not just a product of an election. In politics, dissent amongst colleagues is par for the course and plotting for the advancement of one candidate or another a regular occurrence. Normally, whether from one's own vantage point or through friends, one can see what is going on. But, in this case, I failed at the time to sense the depth of feeling or the threat that it posed to party, let alone national, unity. What hurts most is that these were people I had worked with closely over the years, and whom I had implicitly trusted. So why, in this way, would they change their stance?

Now that I am able to look more closely, I can see that there are generic reasons why this might arise; reasons that can occur in any political system. The post of president is not to be taken lightly and throughout my twelve years as head of state I did my very best to uphold the values that it stands for. I knew at the outset that there would be tough decisions to make and that not everyone would agree. Much as I always hoped that mature politicians would respect these decisions without taking personal offence, or seeking revenge, I also knew that sometimes they would carry their wounds with them. I can see now that this was indeed the case.

Preferment

One obvious source of contention that confronts any political leader on a regular basis is in the allocation of responsibilities. In my own case, for the good of the country, it was my task to select the best possible team of ministers. In doing this, it is necessary to take account of not only an individual's inherent skills and competence, but also how these qualities will match those of other members of the government team. It is also necessary to take a longer-term view, anticipating, like a game of chess, who might later move into a more commanding position. The fact is that ministerial posts are not all of equal weighting – although all are in themselves important for the country – and fellow politicians will be quick to calculate the possible implications of any change. It is hard, for instance, to imagine the appointment of a president who has not previously had firsthand experience of managing the nation's finances. To be specific, Danny Faure was in that position for the best part of a decade and it was fitting that he should (following the retirement in 2010 of Joseph Belmont, the former holder of the post) assume the title of vice-president. I worked closely with him to bring in essential reforms and then to steer our way through the global financial crisis and I could not have wished at the time for a more loyal or competent partner. But, once most of these reforms had been completed, I thought it was time to make a few changes in my team of ministers.

In particular, I could see merit in changing the departmental leadership in matters of finance. This was not only because I wanted to give the vice-president wider experience in government, but also because I had a growing concern that the management of finance had become too entrenched. Apart from the minister himself, his senior advisers had been in post for too long. It seemed to me that they were beginning to act as an independent arm of government, even to the point of making unreported decisions. The result was that I asked Danny Faure to step down (in favour of new responsibilities) and in his place I appointed a widely acknowledged financial expert, Pierre Laporte, to take over as the new minister. Laporte was well qualified to do so, having worked previously for the IMF and then as Governor of the Central Bank of Seychelles. He would not disagree with my definition that he was a technocrat rather than a politician, which, apart from his proven expertise in this field, had the advantage that he could not be seen as usurping the political pecking order.

I explained my reasons for appointing Laporte and reaffirmed with Danny Faure that he was still the frontrunner to take over from me when the time came. My belief was that in giving him responsibilities for youth activities in the country, in addition to his vice-presidential position, he would become better known amongst an important section of the electorate. It would also relieve me of some of my own responsibilities, enabling me to concentrate more directly on strategic matters. Perhaps inevitably, though, the move was misinterpreted in terms of how it might affect the future issue of succession.

The decision to determine who should run as the party candidate for the presidency rests with the party itself, although it was highly unlikely, as the democratically elected president, that my own recommendation would have been questioned. I was in no doubt about who it should be. I had appointed Danny Faure as vice-president with good reason and he was in pole position for future leadership. Political pundits, however, like to suggest their own names and a popular choice was the up-and-coming Jean-Paul Adam. I shared the view that Adam had enormous potential but he was not sufficiently experienced to be brought forward at that stage. The best I could do, with a view to giving Faure the strongest possible team when he came to choose his ministers, was to enable Adam to gain more experience in financial matters. It was for this reason that, when the present minister responsible for finance, Pierre Laporte, resigned in order to take up an overseas post, I brought in Adam as his replacement. Assuming that Danny Faure became the next president, Jean-Paul Adam would still be young enough to follow in his footsteps at a later date.

For all my good intentions, however, people read into this a different motive, a situation that was hardly helped by the unfortunate appearance of a misguided press report. In early 2015 I had agreed to be interviewed by a journalist from a Mauritian newspaper. Interviews of this sort are quite commonplace and the tone of the questions was reasonable in itself. However, for one reason or another, the journalist misinterpreted some of my comments about the future leadership of the country. In particular, it was inferred that Jean-Paul Adam was more popular than Danny Faure within Parti Lepep, and that it was probable he would be chosen as my successor. Most people realized that the incident was the kind of thing that can happen when dealing with the press, accepting the fact that these were certainly not my words, nor my intention. I had never said anything before then to indicate otherwise. But it seems that the incident was not forgotten and conspiracy theorists were quick to alight on the fact that I had appointed Adam as Finance Minister, a post previously held by Faure, interpreting it in their own way as further evidence that he was really the favoured candidate. In such circumstances, the truth can too easily be lost amidst unfounded allegations; and, once lost, it becomes all too hard to recover.

Favours

A second source of contention is also part and parcel of holding the post of president. In any political system, the individual in the most senior post is seen to be in control of the purse strings and all the main levers of power. It is an exaggerated view of how much power even a president really possesses. But this is what people believe and, as such, individuals would sometimes come to my office to ask for favours. 'President', they might say, 'there is some vacant land owned by the government which I could put to good use. It is currently contributing nothing and it would not be unreasonable to transfer it to me for a nominal amount'. Or, 'President, I am a generous donor of funds for your party, and I think the time has come for me to be a government minister'. Readers would be surprised to learn how often this kind of request is made and, even more so, if they knew that such demands might come from those who are not only undeserving but who really ought to know better.

Another ploy that was used at times was to ask me to intervene in the planning process. Why, they would ask, could I not reverse a planning decision that had prevented a particular piece of development? Or why could I not overrule the decision of a government body, say, to release an outer island for development by a prominent individual? I would point out, unambiguously, that decisions are taken for good reason, sometimes to protect a sensitive environment or because it was not appropriate for other reasons. I would also point out that it would not be right for me to use my powers in this way and that due process must always be followed.

Perhaps naively, I hoped that, whether in acquiring land or perverting the course of the planning process, the person(s) involved would understand why I acted as I did but, instead, in a very few cases it became a matter of personal animosity and would re-surface later as a source of revenge. To enflame a situation, there were also times when the incident was reported in the media: someone, for instance, might have overheard a conversation, or the person making the request had been indiscreet. Even though no land actually changed hands, the story itself would be enough to arouse public concern that this kind of concession was a common occurrence, making it all the more important that I could demonstrate the consistency of my own position and put it in perspective.

The same applies when an individual seems to think that they can buy a political office. Perhaps there are countries where this is so, but Seychelles should not be one of them. I can recall a case where, not only was the request very brazen but the person in question could not possibly have performed satisfactorily the duties of a government minister. He had already attained a place in the party hierarchy which was not deserved and which I duly removed. Political parties are always in need of funds but certainly not at any price. The answer in such cases – whether for advancement in government or political party – has to be 'no'. But for those who refuse to hear the adverse outcome, that might not be the end of it, leading to resentment and even the transfer of donations from one party to another. So be it: one has to deal with these things as they arise, but always with probity.

Predecessors

In addition to issues resulting from the appointment of ministers and from the refusal to release government land or to bestow political positions on an illicit basis, there is a third area of potential contention that is inherent in the post of president. The fact is that I was not the first but the third president in our post-independence history, and I always felt that it was my duty to respect the work of my predecessors and to seek continuity where possible. James Mancham was the nation's founding president, assuming office in 1976 but removed after just one year in the coup in which I myself played a part. Along with others, I believed that the kind of change that was needed to unify the country and to address the needs of the majority of the population would not happen under his leadership. He led a different party with its own values and aims and it was not clear how these would change things sufficiently. The result is that he was ousted when he was on an overseas visit and I was part of that process. People still ask how, as a strong advocate of democracy, I could have participated in such an undemocratic action. The question is fair and I can only repeat what I have said many times before.

From the outset, I was ready to play my part in improving the lives of ordinary Seychellois

As a young man, then aged 33, I was already convinced that change was necessary. I was drawn into politics because of this belief and if a coup was the only way, I was willing to support it. To understand, if not to condone, this action, it is important to set it in the context of newly independent African nations in the 1970s. It was a turbulent period, sharpened by the ideological divide of the Cold War, when, after years of colonial rule, socialist revolutions were not unusual. Not only that, but the Western powers seemed to accept this kind of sudden change as an inevitable feature of the post-colonial process. When the new regime was announced in June 1977, France was quick to acknowledge the new regime, followed closely by the UK. In turn, the United States had no problem in negotiating with President René for continued possession and use of its satellite tracking station on Seychelles territory. What was politically acceptable then might well not be so now, but that is how it was and I would not wish to deny my part in the process. There was time enough, when the dust settled, for nations like Seychelles to evolve as it has done.

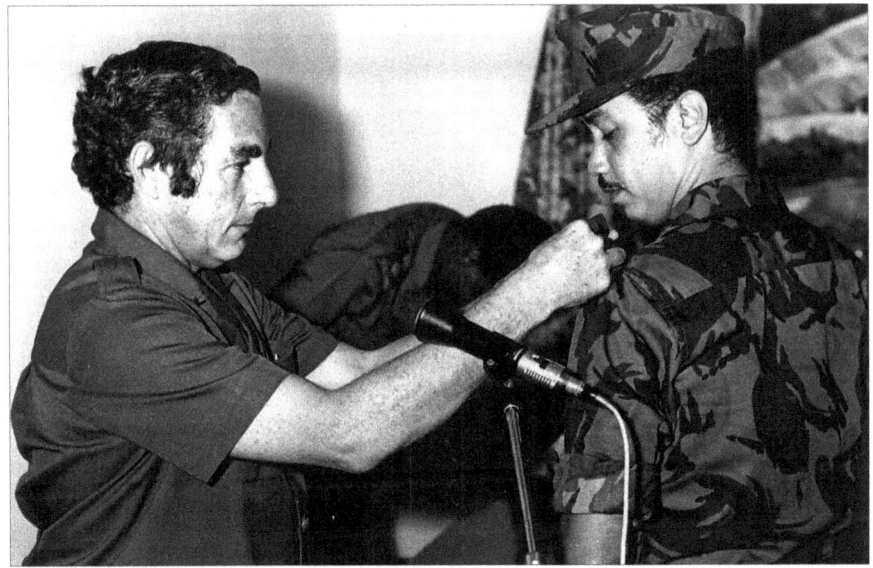

As a young man in the 1970s, serving under President René, radical change in our newly independent nation seemed to me the right way forward

So it was that, in the aftermath of the coup, Mancham went into exile for fifteen years, only returning to Seychelles with the re-introduction of multi-party politics. Like others in the ruling party at the time, I was unsure what his eventual return would mean for the country. It was clear from the moment he stepped from the aircraft that he still enjoyed enormous support, and he was received like a returning hero. In the following months, however, in the face of the practical tasks of preparing to stand in the coming election, some of this euphoria subsided and, in the event, he was unable to topple the ruling party. But what impressed me most was that I could see that he genuinely wanted to heal old wounds and contribute to reconciliation. This is why, in my own presidency, I treated him with due respect and asked him, from time to time, to represent me at overseas events, in effect in the role of an unofficial ambassador. In the common interest of serving our country, we found an effective way to work together.

The circumstances surrounding the second president, France Albert René, were, of course, very different. He and I shared the same political beliefs and I served under him for the entire twenty-seven years of his presidency. René was a strong and determined leader who, more than anyone, was responsible for the far-reaching changes that resulted in this period. I was loyal to him throughout his presidency and he, in turn, acknowledged my potential to take over from him when he stood down in 2004. Many people in Seychelles had grown up with the same president, and it was only to be expected that they would now ask whether I would carry on in the same way or strike out along a different path. In fact, if one looks at any political system, there is no single outcome in this kind of situation, even if the successor comes from the same political party; some successors carry on as before while others turn their backs on the past and strike out in a different direction.

I worked closely with President René throughout the twenty-seven years of his presidency

I was always very clear of my own stance. Until I stood for election in my own right, I saw myself as working broadly within the terms of René's remaining mandate. I was new to the post and the transitional period would give me time to review the situation and assess future options.

And so it was that each week I would meet the previous president and we would discuss the issues of the day. After the election of 2006 I felt free to pursue my own mandate. Of course, I would still meet René on a regular basis and listen carefully to what he had to say but I was now ready to go beyond that, especially in terms of reforming the country's finances and economic system. With the ending of the Cold War more than a decade previously, the world had changed and there would be no more baling out by countries with a shared socialist ideology; the day of relying on deficit budgets had surely come to an end and Seychelles would have to look after itself.

René and I were not always in agreement on some matters, especially the need for radical financial reform, and, in retrospect, it must have been difficult for him to come to terms with the reality of turning in a new direction. Perhaps it was even more difficult than I had realized at the time and it should not have been a surprise to me that he developed a close relationship with Danny Faure, who, increasingly, he regarded as his protegé. In turn, I can see now that it was René, not me, who my successor regarded as his true mentor. In his inauguration speech in 2016, President Faure's acknowledgement of the debt owed to René could not have been clearer:

> *Each one of us has been inspired by different people, by different personalities. Me, I draw my inspiration from President René. Today I would like to say a Big Thank You to him. His principles, such as liberty and social justice which fuelled our struggle for Independence and the creation of a more fair society.*[69]

In retrospect, that also helps to explain why, when I was contemplating running again for the presidency in 2015, René, to my surprise and disappointment, advised against it. In brief, he said that he did not agree with some of my policies and actions and that I should stand down in favour of his own preferred candidate, Danny Faure. This ran counter to what we had previously agreed, which was that I should hand over part way through the post-2015 term of office, to allow my successor time to lead the country before himself facing the electorate (just as I had done myself between 2004 and 2006). It hardly helped that he expressed his preference in the presence of Danny Faure, who at the time made no attempt to question René's decision. Reflecting on the occasion, I gained a strong sense that the matter had been discussed previously between the two of them and that it was, in their minds, a *fait accompli*. Thus, at the earliest opportunity, I met again with the former president, not so much to question his strongly held view but to ask why he had expressed it in front of his preferred successor. I saw the way it was done as discourteous in the least, and harmful to my authority, but I am afraid that my concerns fell on deaf ears. There is an African saying that one should never force a lion against a wall so that it has only one way to move. Like the cornered lion, I also knew there was only one response. Determined not to be forced to concede in this way, I was by then doubly convinced that I would stand again at the next election and, no less, that I would win. If I were subsequently to stand down and nominate my successor, it would be a result of free will and not under duress.

The episode left me with a sour taste but, more than that, it alerted me for the first time to the stirrings of a conspiracy. Though not yet a tsunami, I took seriously the warnings of this early sign of turbulence. A rift was developing at the highest level, one that only really opened up after I stood down in 2016. Perhaps, when it did, I should not have been surprised, let alone disappointed. I had for so long thought better of this exclusive circle where now I could sense ominous signs of betrayal.

In mitigation, I know that René's health was failing at the time and that he was not the man he was. I fear that people close to him, might well have taken advantage of his weakness, persuading him to say and do things that he would not have done when he was stronger. One can only speculate, of course, about what really happened in his dying days, but he was certainly a very different man from the one I had known for so many years.

Boundaries

Finally, in mapping out some of the main challenges for a president, one must always be aware of changes in the surrounding political landscape. In the preceding two presidential and constituency elections, it had been a familiar scene. On the one side was Parti Lepep and on the other the main opposition party, led by Wavel Ramkalawan; there would always be a few independent candidates but these had not in the past really changed the balance. Ramkalawan was an old adversary who had yet to taste success but kept coming back for more. The two of us were tried and tested opponents, with strong differences of view but also a common respect for the democratic process and the traditions of the country.

This was all familiar enough but, by the time of the elections of 2015 and 2016, the situation was changing in various ways. I was fortunate once again to be representing Parti Lepep, which was an effective campaigning force and had won every election to date, and I was confident I could win again. In other respects, with a realignment of political party boundaries across the nation as a whole, there was a difference. For one thing, by the time of the re-run of the presidential election towards the end of 2015, Ramkalawan could count on the support of several smaller parties which, in the following year was formalized through the creation of a new party, Linyon Demokratik Seselwa (LDS). The other, and more immediate change, was the entry of a former Parti Lepep stalwart, Patrick Pillay, campaigning now on his own platform. Unlike some of the other opposition candidates, Pillay was an experienced politician who, we all knew, could attract a sizeable number of his own supporters. We were, indeed, entering new territory for the national elections.

I had known Pillay for years and, as a former Parti Lepep member, he had held ministerial as well as ambassadorial posts. Indeed, I had helped him in a personal sense by appointing him as our nation's diplomatic representative in London, at a time when for family reasons he especially wanted to be there. When Pillay subsequently returned to his home in Seychelles, I thought that, after a long and eventful career, he would then choose to retire in peace. Far from it, and before long I heard that Pillay had plans to form a new political party and that he was in discussion with another former government minister, to whom he offered the prospective post of vice-president. The political landscape was, indeed, changing.

With the presidential elections in prospect towards the end of 2015, Patrick Pillay gathered his forces around his new party, Lalyans Seselwa, confident that he could make a major impact. He was not at first prepared to align with the party of the leading oppositional figure, Wavel Ramkalawan. It was known that there was no love lost between the two, and that a lasting alliance was always in doubt. In any case, Pillay thought he was more popular than he really was and tried to go it alone. It proved to be a hard-fought campaign, marked by personal animosity, in which Pillay and his followers variously accused me of betraying my own supporters and of being less than honest in my management of government funds. None of the allegations had substance but they succeeded in souring the atmosphere.

Another unwanted feature of the election campaign was the adoption by some of Pillay's supporters of the words of a song, 'Pile pil lo li', written by a local performer. The song carried the crude message of 'stamping them down' (meaning, of course, myself and Parti Lepep). It is hard to exaggerate the significance of this shift into territory never before known in political dialogue within Seychelles, urging the electorate to engage in a chant that could only incite hatred and aggression. In my view, this insulted the dignity of our people, reducing the level of debate to that of venomous lies and barely veiled violence. It ran counter to everything that had, in the face of any differences, for so long dignified our country; it smeared in an offensive way the very essence of Creole culture. Clearly, it dismissed the sentiments of the Constitution, which spoke so proudly of peace and harmony:

> *Aware and proud that as descendants of different races we have learnt to live together as one Nation under God and can serve as an example for the harmonious multi-racial society;*
>
> *Recognizing the inherent dignity and the equal and inalienable rights of all members of the human family as the foundation for freedom, justice, welfare. fraternity, peace and unity;*
>
> *Reaffirming that these rights include the rights of the individual to life, liberty and the pursuit of happiness free from all types of discrimination;*
>
> *Considering that these rights are most effectively maintained and protected in a democratic society where all powers of Government spring from the will of the people...*[70]

During the campaign, good Seychellois citizens were lured across a line which could only nourish the seeds of bitterness and dissent. Before long, the call to 'stamp them down' was heard not only at political rallies but in the streets and, worst of all, from the mouths of young people in schools and in the neighbourhoods. Young and old alike voiced the chant. The sentiment was insidious and undermined everything for which Seychelles stood. It amounted to a call to take what one wanted by any means, at the price of respect for one's elders and anyone who held different views. It saw the emergence of racist accusations in public debate and everyday life, something which, through our respect for each other, we had thankfully been spared from in the past. And I believe it contributed in no small way to the spread of bad behaviour and even criminality in our country. Perhaps the full effects of the provocative campaign message had not been intended at the time and it had been seen as no more than a cheap election gimmick. But the evil genie had been released from the bottle and it would prove to be no easy task to put it back. Responsible leaders should never have condoned such an action; our people deserved better.

Identity

There was a completeness in it, something solid like a principle.[71]

It seemed, at last, that I might find time to read and reflect, as well as promote the Blue Economy

By the time I stepped down from high office I had served my country in government for close to four decades. It had never been easy, but always rewarding, and I could look back on so many worthwhile changes. Now that I was free of day-to-day commitments, I could be forgiven for thinking that I might at last find time to reflect on my career and, if asked, offer my experience to the next generation of politicians and aspiring young leaders. And, if an opportunity arose to carry forward the message of the

Blue Economy, I was more than willing to do so. In these different ways, I looked forward to a peaceful though still fulfilling life. I could spend more time with those near and dear to me, and, who knows, I might even be able to indulge my love of poetry? I also had plans to write my memoirs, telling the story of an eventful life. The future would be different from what I had known in the past but I was relaxed about what it had to bring; a new chapter was about to begin.

When I stood down as president, I was prepared to make a new contribution to the development of Seychelles

Of course, in the febrile political environment at the time, perhaps it was too much to hope for a quiet and dignified exit. Bad feeling had been stirred up in the course of the elections and, even though some of the most vitriolic and ill-founded comments originated with just a few individuals, and were not necessarily directed only to me, I knew that some criticism would come my way. With so many allegations flying around, it seemed sensible to keep one's head down.

One might ask whether all of this really mattered. After all, as a seasoned politician I was used to dealing with criticism, and when it is constructive it is always important to respond. In this case, though, it felt very different from anything experienced in the past. There was a ferocity about it and a sense that the instigators were prepared to say anything to make their case, regardless of whether there was any truth in their allegations. Some of the comments were clearly designed to hurt me, and others, personally, but what was most injurious was the fact that they were, quite simply, wrong. I knew that was the case but could I be sure that others knew it too? People were saying things that, if allowed to rest, would undermine everything I had done with good intent in my long career. My own character and reputation, and those of my friends and colleagues around me, as well as the very integrity of Seychelles, were all under fire. The slurs had to be rebutted, the record put straight.

Refuting Allegations

To unmask falsehood, and bring truth to light.[72]

Over the period of these various attacks, I can see that they were directed to a number of different targets but in all cases I found myself included in the line of fire. There were, first of all, those accusations which went right back to the removal of the founding president and subsequent events, implicating me as a member of the government in the ensuing years. A second category included unsubstantiated allegations that a large sum of state money could not be accounted for, the suggestion being that I was personally responsible and had maybe diverted funds into my own account. Another flurry of attacks questioned my close relationship with the United Arab Emirates, inferring that I had benefited personally from the arrangement. And, at a more domestic level, the building that accommodated the Jj Spirit Foundation (the charity I set up with the former vice-president, Joseph Belmont) became the subject of spurious allegations and outright lies. It is time for me now to present my side of the story. In refuting the various attacks on my character, some will maintain that what I am saying is incorrect. Of course, everyone is entitled to their opinion and I can do no more than set out my version of events, based on the facts. The important thing for me is that my conscience is clear.

Guilty by association?

To be fair, most of the comments about the Second Republic, the period following the removal of the founding president, were directed not so much at me but at James Mancham's successor, France Albert René. But I was an enthusiastic young member of the new regime and I am more than prepared to justify my own actions and the part I played in the social and economic transformation of Seychelles.

As I have already explained in earlier chapters, at the time the British left our islands the people were still (as they had always been in the colonial era) deeply divided between the 'haves' and 'have nots'. Poverty was rife and radical changes were long overdue to redress the timeworn situation. Change of this sort would not have been possible without a new approach. In common with other young nations in the 1970s, socialism seemed to offer the way forward and, under René's leadership, this was the route we followed. As one of the 'have nots' who had been held back by the old system I was more than ready to contribute to change. The prospect of removing barriers for all and creating a land of fairness and opportunity could not have been more compelling. For a young man with his life ahead of him the choice was clear and, to this day, I do not regret my decision to join the new government. Quite simply, I wanted to see a better future for my country.

I honestly believed that society could be changed in the ways intended without a single life being lost and without the needless use of force. Although there would be some who opposed the changes – those who had most to lose in the reversal of power and wealth – I thought a peaceful transition was possible. In the event, some of those who disagreed most with the new regime chose of their own volition to leave the country voluntarily and start a new life elsewhere. Unfortunately, there were others whose land was confiscated and given little choice to leave with only their personal belongings. There was little room for dissent. President René was a strong leader with a clear vision of what his government wanted to achieve. That has never been seriously disputed but in the more recent climate of blame and calls for retribution some of his methods have been questioned. In particular, it is recalled that opposition to his leadership was not to be countenanced and if he could rid himself of oppositional figures he would.

As I was a member of his successive governments throughout the twenty-seven years of his presidency, it is understandable that my own role should now be questioned too. In response, I am totally clear about two things: I agreed with the overall aims of the new regime, but I always believed they could be achieved peaceably and with a respect for commonly held human values. I was a proud member of René's government but, especially in the early days, there were more powerful figures in the inner circle. In those early days, I was still young and relatively inexperienced and not necessarily a party to key decisions. Things were often done by René himself or with one or two close advisers, without informing fellow ministers. I watched and I spoke my mind when issues relevant to my own responsibilities arose, but it was not until I was a senior minister, prior to assuming the leadership myself, that I could assert more fully my personal values and priorities.

Over such a long period of government it is inevitable that some decisions in that period would be questionable. I was one of those, for instance, who had serious doubts about the hasty introduction of the National Youth Service, which required all young people to spend two years away from home so that they could be immersed in socialist doctrine. Borrowing from the experience of other socialist countries, René saw it as an attempt to cleanse the next generation of bourgeois family values and overnight to dismantle the class system. My concern at the time was that this very radical idea had not been fully thought through and discussed, and the human and physical infrastructure to make it work was not in place. There were other ministers who took the same view, but René would brook no delay and pressed ahead regardless. The new scheme worked for some but by no means all, and the requirement for young people of an impressionable age to turn their backs on all they had previously learned in their homes and schools was a step too far. Rome was not built in a day and the socialist utopia would take even longer.

In personal terms, I could see that both my sons, who had until then grown up in a traditional family structure, were adversely affected by the experience and, tragically, the unhappiness created led directly to the untimely demise of the elder of the two. The pain of this terrible loss is still with me and always will be. In any government, individual ministers will have their own reservations about certain aspects of what is being done but, within reason, they will be prepared to accommodate these in the wider interest. For me this wider interest was the process of transformation that was being achieved. Thus, while I admired the president in most respects it was only natural that I would also have doubts about some of his alleged actions. I am not claiming that I was unaware of rumours of individuals who had been reprimanded for not following the party line, and in some cases of people who had disappeared; all of this was, in any case, common knowledge at the time. But I can honestly say that there were certain things that I did not know about at the time, which I was never asked to approve; nor was I expected to condone any unlawful action.

Politics is a pragmatic business and, on a day-to-day basis, one has to balance the good with the bad. I knew that René was much loved by a majority of the people and I was one of those who firmly believed that the changes he was making were for the good of the country, even if I wondered whether the means in all cases justified the ends. Moreover, I also believed that my own balanced view was widely shared by others. I was constantly loyal to the president while, at the same time, aware that not everyone agreed with everything he did. Recognition of this ambivalence is reflected in the overwhelmingly laudatory tribute I wrote, following his passing in February 2019:

> *An icon of the Seychellois nation has passed away today, 27th February 2019.*
>
> *A foremost son of Seychelles is no longer with us. An era has passed.*
>
> *I join his family and the people of Seychelles in grieving the death of President France Albert René. His demise leaves a great void amongst us.*
>
> *France Albert René was my mentor, my tutor and my inspiration. To him I owe my political career and experience. His were the hands that guided me through many tumultuous years and helped me surmount countless obstacles. He gave me confidence and faith in myself. He helped forge my principles and beliefs to which I have remained true and faithful to this day.*
>
> *To quote a great and accomplished man of the 17th century, enshrined in history, 'If I have seen further, it is by standing upon*

the shoulders of giants'. Giants such as France Albert René.

France Albert René was an indomitable fighter. He believed in a society of social justice, of equality, of access to health, housing and education. He fought tirelessly against bigotry, racial division and hatred.

In the process, and throughout his work and presidency, he touched every one of us – in one way or another. Acclaimed by many – including those far beyond the shores of our homeland – and reviled by some, France Albert René left no one indifferent to the man he was and to the principles he advocated. Principles which are at the core of human values and rights.

Regardless of one's feelings towards him, his achievements far outweighed any shortcomings that, as any human being, he may have had.

France Albert René will be remembered as one of the founding fathers of the First Republic and the architect of the Second and Third Republic. In this regard, he will live on in our memories.

His lasting legacy will be that of a freedom fighter and a liberator. A compassionate and simple man, who shunned publicity, he fought passionately for the Independence of Seychelles and thereafter for our Liberation from the last vestiges of colonialism. He believed firmly in the unity of our brothers and sisters on the African continent, and in the universality of humankind. He never tired or failed to advocate those principles. And he gained the respect and admiration of many.

History will judge him fairly and the Seychellois people will judge him right.

> *In this hour of national grief, let us pay our respects to this towering figure of our modern history and mourn him in peace and reverence.*
>
> *I offer my deepest condolences to the family of President France Albert René and all their loved ones and pray that they be granted the courage to surmount their great loss.*

'History will judge him fairly', I said, and perhaps it is still too soon to attempt such a judgement. But, to the extent that I am myself being questioned by his record, it is only right that I affirm my belief that René took the country in the right direction. His towering achievement in transforming life in Seychelles in a single generation is beyond question. But I suspect that history might probe more fully whether he went beyond the bounds of his presidential office, using some methods to which I have already alluded. The use of violence to quell any signs of opposition cannot be condoned. Likewise, the confiscation of land – sometimes by needlessly brutal means and driven by personal vendettas – was an obvious misuse of power that cannot in any sense be defended. It is a sad fact that being in control for such a long period encourages a belief that leads to a sense of entitlement, a belief that there are no limits to what one is free to do; this why my measure to limit the period of a presidency to two terms is so important. It is also undeniable that he came under the influence of a number of so-called advisers who sought personal financial gain. As I have already mentioned, especially in his later years when he was no longer president and in poor health, I believe he was particularly vulnerable to the unjustified and self-promoting demands of others.

Because of what he did for the country, most Seychellois rightly remain loyal to his memory – one only has to recall the dedications at his state funeral – but external observers are less guarded in their views. For instance, flouting normal rules of diplomatic protocol, David Fischer, a former American ambassador in Seychelles reported (after he left his post in 1985) in one of the opposition newspapers that the country was a haven for financial transactions by arms dealers and a staging post for drug trafficking. Readers were reminded that a Seychellois exile in London, who was compiling a list of illegal transactions, was murdered before he could release his next revelations. And Fischer put his name to a lurid report claiming that:

> *In late 1984, in the US, the New Jersey police found the mutilated bodies of two local drug-traffickers, apparent victims of a gangland killing. One of the two had in his pocket an address book which contained the name and private phone number of President France Albert René.*[73]

A more measured account is to be found in a refereed article in a recent academic journal, in which the author paints another gloomy picture of René's record:

> *Under René, political patronage, repression, cronyism and corruption amplified. René transformed Seychelles into an authoritarian state only to morph it under international pressure late in his rule to one with a multi-party and democratic entity.*[74]

There is further reference in the article to links with the American mafia and René himself is likened in his later years to a godfather figure in the ruling party.

These are damaging observations and, whether they stand up to close interrogation or not, they undoubtedly harm the reputation of Seychelles and, indeed, of those who were part of the René regime. That is why, when I became president, I was quick to take action to tackle corruption, to build a proper system of intelligence gathering, to add weight to the war against drugs, and to target issues like money laundering. These were all areas which I could see had been allowed to drift. And, as I show in the following section, it is why I believe there is still more work to be done.

Follow the money

The opposition parties, with their newly-won majority in the National Assembly in late-2016, lost no time in making their presence felt. They clearly wanted to achieve a few quick wins, not so much at that stage by pressing for new policies but rather through a negative campaign to try to smear the record of the previous regime. It was a middle-term strategy, which I believe was designed to destroy the credibility of the ruling party as a way for the opposition to improve its position in subsequent elections. In the course of this process, I became a personal target of some of their allegations, amongst which the most sustained was an accusation that certain items of state funds could not be accounted for.

The quest for the 'missing money' quickly turned into a witch-hunt, embroiling not only myself but also my most trusted advisers. As well as formal channels of enquiry, social media provided a platform for all kinds of lurid interpretations that were totally unfounded but none the less damaging to my reputation. In one sense, attacks from the political opposition and individuals who were not in command of the facts were not a cause for surprise. Instead, what hurt me most was that a number of former political colleagues (some of whom I had mistakenly thought were also friends) were not slow to jump on the bandwagon. I found myself in an unenviable position. Facts were in short supply and there were few, if any, of my accusers who seemed interested to find out what really happened.

In fact, there were two unrelated strands to this assault on my character. One goes back to the tail end of René's presidency, in 2002, when I was then holding the office of Minister of Finance. After years of deficit budgets, the country was in desperate straits, unable to pay for vital imports and on the verge of bankruptcy. In one of a succession of benevolent gestures, our friends in the UAE stepped in with a bailout amounting to US$ 50 million. Because I was the responsible minister for finance at the time, my critics erroneously assumed that I could explain what happened to this large sum. But I was not in a position to do so. When the money was received in Seychelles, President René immediately requested that I transfer it to an account with the Bank of Baroda in London. From that point on, he and his economic adviser, Mukesh Valabhji, took control of the account and I had no further involvement. In addition to earlier rebuttals of what I was purported to have done with the money, I have recently explained this to members of the Anti-Corruption Commission. The ball is now well and truly in their court.

The second accusation of missing money is equally based on assertions rather than evidence. This line of criticism all began shortly after I took up the post of president in 2004. I would meet the then Governor of the Central Bank on a regular basis and in the course of conversation he expressed concern that decisions he had made in confidence were being leaked before they could be implemented. Especially given the sensitivity of the financial situation at the time, the importance of this could not be overstated. But that was not all and, on closer consideration, I became convinced that a similar breach of confidentiality was taking place in my own office. Action had to be taken, and I agreed with Governor's suggestion that he should contact a firm of security consultants (based in Ireland and with a credible record of international commissions) with which he was already acquainted. Recognizing the urgency of the situation, contact was made and the designated experts soon arrived in Seychelles. Just as we had suspected, an examination of our respective offices revealed a number of concealed listening devices. Two were removed from the Governor's office and three from mine, as well as one from the vice-president's office (which, until shortly before then, I had occupied).

The bugs were duly removed but it led me to question not only why my conversations were being monitored but also to ask what else needed attention. To coin a phrase, rumours that something was rotten at the heart of the state had to be addressed. Gone was the day when this was the responsibility of others; it was time for me in my new role to confront the situation directly and take appropriate action. After sifting through the evidence, I concluded that four issues had to be urgently addressed.

- One obvious area of concern was the domestic security system. Relying on bugs in key offices was hardly the basis for inspiring trust in the government. Who was monitoring them and for what purpose?

- A second problem was the absence of a formal intelligence system for the nation as a whole. We had no systematic way of knowing what foreign powers in the region were engaged in nor, when it came to it later, how the pirates off the coast of Somalia were operating. Every nation must have its own intelligence system but ours was virtually non-existent.

- Thirdly, particularly as a result of the collapse of the Soviet Union and the outflow of funds released from state assets, Seychelles had acquired an unenviable reputation for money laundering. Yet nothing had been done to improve the situation. We were regarded as falling well short of international standards.

- And, finally, the illicit importation of heroin was threatening the very fabric of the country. Huge sums of money were being made by a few, regardless of the injurious effects on individuals. Any one of these issues was of enormous importance in a small country but, taken together, the impact was potentially devastating – for the people within the country and for our international reputation. Action had to be taken without further delay.

Given our satisfaction with the discreet and effective response of the Irish consultants, the Governor and I decided to ask them to make a business case for a more comprehensive commission. Their contacts and the range of expertise that they could call on were impressive and highly professional, and we agreed that they should take a lead on further work. Our faith in this firm has never been in question and we enjoyed a positive working relationship. As a result of their findings, important changes were soon introduced, in the form of a 'fit for purpose' intelligence system, a new institution to tackle the problem of money laundering, and a complete change in the way we dealt with drug enforcement. The measures that were taken are explained in an earlier chapter of this book, in which I describe this initiative as one of the main elements of my legacy. Critics would later say that the fees for our consultants were exorbitant but the work they were undertaking was highly specialized and based on experience of international best practice. If allowed to run its course, Seychelles would have been able to demonstrate watertight systems and to be held in high regard by the rest of the world.

Sadly, that was not to be the case. It was as if the opposition parties, with their newly-won majority in the country's parliament, saw more to be gained for themselves in dismantling what I had been able to achieve. Chaired by the new leader of the majority party, Wavel Ramkalawan, the Finance and Public Accounts Committee was asked by the National Assembly to investigate the use of state funds for the above activities. Was the money paid to the Irish consultants a proper use of public funds? Accountability is one thing but, in this case, a basic flaw in the process was soon apparent. The subject matter of the inquiry required a degree of confidentiality that should have been recognized. It was in the national interest to be discreet about certain transactions, including some of the related monetary details. However, the kind of understanding I had hoped for was not apparent.

I sensed from the outset – before any evidence had been heard – that it had already been decided that funds had been misappropriated and that my own character was in question. The whole tone of the inquiry was vengeful and witnesses called from my office were treated with disrespect. In one instance, an inappropriate question was asked that could have resulted in the release of secret information that was safeguarded by law. More disappointing than the nature of the inquiry itself, however, was the apparent determination of some members of the new Executive to unravel the measures I had put in place. The impact of these actions was not at all in the interests of the country. I can see that some of this reversal has since been corrected by the incoming government but the damage in the interim was inestimable.

Although the new intelligence system was all but complete, with the necessary equipment already purchased, any further progress was curtailed. Much of the work of operating the system had been handled by the Financial Intelligence Unit (FIU) but national security was now to be launched as a separate operation. Even more damaging, the details of the contractual arrangement were leaked through the above committee, with the immediate effect of undermining the arrangements. No nation provides the rest of the world with details of its security system, but, due to the clumsy if not malicious handling of the issue by some politicians, Seychelles has proved to be an exception. Perhaps this unfortunate outcome was not entirely intentional – a product more of inexperience – but the effect was the same.

Similarly, on the drugs front, the National Drugs Enforcement Agency (NDEA) was abolished and, in spite of the clear evidence of corruption in the past, responsibility for drug control was handed back to the police. Once that was done, there were no further large hauls of intercepted consignments. And, to complete the process of turning back the clock, the FIU, likewise, was effectively downgraded, making it easier for a fresh flow of illegal transfers of funds to enter the country.

In these different ways, Seychelles slipped back to the status of an offshore haven for illicit activities and the nation's reputation in the international community was damaged. Our small nation, which had done so much to win the admiration of other countries for its work in these fields, was now blacklisted. So much good work was undone in the name of political expediency. The funds in question had not been misappropriated, as was wrongly contended, and, as I have shown elsewhere, a separate account with a balance of US$5 million had been set up with the Central Bank to manage payments in an appropriate way. Any withdrawals had to be jointly signed by the head of the FIU, by the Secretary-General of the President's Office, and by the Minister of Finance, and only then with my approval. All of this, in any case, took place under the watchful eye of the Governor of the Central Bank. Of course, the 'missing' contracts were in safe hands too but, for obvious reasons of state security, these could not be made widely available; one would have hoped that this would have been understood by those who were by then making decisions. The outcome was that valuable progress was reversed and one can only ask why this was done; the only beneficiaries are those who stand to gain from what should always be branded as illegal activities. At a recent international conference on the Blue Economy, one participant in the audience asked how it was that so many good ideas on the subject could emanate from such a corrupt nation. He was subsequently challenged outside the session on the accusatory point but if that is how Seychelles is now viewed it is a matter of regret for us all. Such accusations reflect badly on the nation as a whole.

To cap it all, the Auditor-General undertook his own investigation and the findings showed conclusively that I and my colleagues were totally exonerated on any suspicion of fraud and corruption. I had hoped to receive an apology from the investigating committee but that was not forthcoming.

The diplomacy of friendship

Diplomatic relations normally proceed on the basis of mutual benefits for two or more parties. It is less a question of one group of people necessarily liking another than of the expediency, say, of nations bound together by security or trade. Very occasionally, however, genuine human ties evolve and the relationship becomes, as well, one of friendship. In such instances, the cause of diplomacy is helped in the process. This is how I believe the link with the United Arab Emirates (UAE) has evolved. The founding president, Sir James Mancham, took the same view, recalling in one of his books how, during a visit in 2011, the Crown Prince of Abu Dhabi described the UAE's relationship with Seychelles as not just a friendship but a love affair.

Against this background it saddens me when an unrepresentative few Seychellois (usually through social media) seek to undermine our relationship with the UAE. This is the view of 'little islanders' who seem unaware of our global context and ignorant of all the help we have received. From the very outset of my presidency, when Seychelles was in a dire economic situation, I have had good reason to be grateful for many gestures of friendship and material support. Whenever they felt they could help, they immediately did so. It was very soon apparent to me that the royal family of the UAE had great affection for our islands and our people, born of the opportunity of a quiet retreat just a few hours away from their own country but also a result of the friendly reception they received as visitors. There was never, as is sometimes inferred in critical postings, any question of gaining control or advantage on their part; nor of personal gain for me and my colleagues. The evidence speaks for itself.

When I could see that our reserves of foreign exchange were perilously low the Crown Prince of the Emirate of Abu Dhabi immediately stepped in; when, on another occasion, we were running out of petrol our friends from the Arab kingdom were quick to offer support; and even when our supply of fresh water was nearly exhausted in a period of drought, they airlifted equipment so that we could install two desalination plants. This kind of relationship has long roots and, before I became president and had ultimate responsibility for finance, they took to heart my view that what we needed most of all to be financially sustainable was investment. As a result, they brought to Mahé the luxury hotel brand, 'Four Seasons', and there are plans for comparable development on the distant Platte Island. Land was bought at Anse à la Mouche and Police Bay, although, in a breach of trust that will not be quickly forgotten, my successor asked the legitimate owners of the land at Police Bay to return it to the Seychelles government. In so doing, I believe a red line was crossed and goodwill and friendship between our two nations was temporarily undermined in the process.

In the company of His Highness Sheikh Khalifa bin Zayed Al Nahyan, President of the UAE, who has been consistently supportive of Seychelles

Time and again I have looked to the UAE for assistance, and always the leaders have been ready to respond. Introducing our economic reforms in 2008 required additional capital and I was grateful to receive on behalf of the government the sum of US$15 million to make the changes possible. In turn, much of our infrastructure is the result of generous grants and donations. The list is long and the benefits enduring: affordable housing on reclaimed land at Perseverance, funded through a US$ 30 million grant and, more recently, funds to enable another affordable housing scheme at Barbarons; a new diagnostic centre for Seychelles Hospital worth US$ 11 million; two electric generators valued at US$ 15 million; a donation of US$ 25 million for equipment to enable renewable energy to be generated from the wind; forty new buses to replace some of the outdated vehicles in the public transport system; IT equipment to improve internet access in all of our schools; a Twin-Otter aircraft to help us patrol our extensive EEZ, and a new coastguard base and five patrol boats to help in our fight against Somalian pirates. And, through a partnership with the Abu Dhabi airline, Etihad, new life was injected into Air Seychelles when it was nearing bankruptcy. Nor was it all a question of big projects, and I can recall fondly

On behalf of the UAE, His Highness Sheikh Mohamed bin Zayed Al Nahyan has not only provided national funding for numerous projects but he has also been a generous personal benefactor to assist Seychelles

the gesture of airlifting two young Seychellois for urgent medical treatment in Abu Dhabi.

In spite of this impressive record, some of our more xenophobic compatriots persist in accusing our friends of ulterior motives. They forget not only what has already been done for our country but also the fact that, with its enormous wealth, the UAE already has all that it wants and has no need to profit from the relationship. In this context, I believe it was in all of our interests to provide some land for the building of residences where the rulers and their families could spend time in our oceanic setting. Not only did this represent a valuable source of investment for us and regular expenditure and employment locally, but it was our way of thanking our friends for their constant support. What is more, far from conceding the land without payment it was always sold at market rates. The late Sir James Mancham has generously acknowledged the wisdom of the action:

> *Well, history has shown what a great move President Michel's gesture was, and that the land was really the foundation of new economic development support for Seychelles.*[77]

The UAE is still deeply committed to further investment and new development to support Seychelles. But, I fear that, while our personal bonds are unbroken, some of the warmth that underpinned the formal relationship between our two nations during my own time in government was eroded by the actions and attitude of my successor. Diplomacy is not all about treaties and trade figures. Friendships contain an immeasurable element of chemistry and that is what seems to have been lost. Fortunately, the excellent relations of the past have been recovered and there are, once again, many good things to celebrate.

A place for charity

Another aspect of my legacy, which has come under the spotlight of spite and mistrust, is a project I pioneered to support the youth of this country. Although it is something to which I have always given my support, the real impetus came from young people themselves. Launched in 2008, I was invited to assume the position of Patron of the non-governmental organisation, which took the name of the Jj Spirit Foundation (derived from my own first name and that of the then vice-president, Joseph Belmont).

Founding members of the Jj Spirit Foundation, the charity I formed with my then vice-president, Joseph Belmont

The Jj Spirit Foundation was dedicated wholly to providing opportunities and activities for young people and was never part of government. Given the level of enthusiasm and the scope for its work, land was acquired at the valuation price and funds were raised for an imposing building on the waterfront in Victoria. The building was named Espace. Some US$ 12 million was needed and US$ 5 million was generously donated by sponsors, the largest amount being US$ 3 million as a personal donation from His Highness Sheikh Mohamed bin Zayed Al Nahyan, Crown Prince of the Emirate of Abu Dhabi and Deputy Supreme Commander of the UAE Armed Forces. That still left a sizeable loan and each year repayments were met through income from rents for office and other space in the large building. The idea was that, once the capital was repaid, the income generated would be available for different projects; this was expected to be possible within just a few more years.

One might have thought that a non-profit-making enterprise for the benefit of young people would enjoy unquestioned support. It was not costing the taxpayers anything, and it made its own contribution to a healthy and productive citizenry for the future. Sadly, goodwill was in short supply in certain quarters and it was not long before the opposition parties and others rallied to fire the first shots. Behind the lines, it was possible that certain members of government were also prepared to undermine the project. I have no doubt that if it were not this it would have been something else designed to harm me, but the specific target in this case was the occupancy of part of the building for government offices and the rent it attracted. It was an excellent space for the Department of Tourism and a valuable source of income for Espace. For their own political interests, however, negative forces were determined to damage the charitable organization.

A confrontation was clearly engineered. Unless the owners of Espace ended the tenancy arrangement with this government department, the opposition parties threatened to use their majority in the National Assembly to block the national budget. In some circles that would be seen as using disproportionate force to achieve a more limited objective. But the fact is that the threat proved effective. I discussed the situation with my colleagues and we were agreed that it could harm the future of Espace if we were to become embroiled in an unseemly dispute that might deter a new cohort of prospective tenants. We were also concerned not to cause embarrassment to our sponsors, who had supported us in good faith. As a result, we decided to ride the wave and end the tenancy with the relevant ministry.

It was a great disappointment to be treated in this way and a sign of how far relations had deteriorated. I was no longer in politics but I was, improperly in my view, harassed and drawn back to the political arena. Unfortunately, this was not the only attempt to damage the charity. At the time of its inception and for the first few years, the charity was eligible to apply for funds from the nation's Corporate Social Responsibility scheme and, on that basis, students were awarded scholarships to study abroad. But, for no good reason, the tap was abruptly turned off and we had to find other ways to enable students already overseas to complete their studies. Once again, I could not help but wonder if the hand of government was at work.

Political pettiness such as the above only strengthened my resolve to make a lasting success of Espace. Our legal right to do so was beyond question and we were soon to be in the process of repackaging our remaining loan so that it could be repaid over a longer period. A new generation of tenants was taking up space released by the Department of Tourism and, given the centrality of the location and the quality of accommodation, I believed that we could view the future with confidence. The Jj Spirit Foundation itself continued to enjoy strong leadership and would soon become part of my own James Michel Foundation. Visitors to Espace could see that my library and museum are located there too and I was proud that, in spite of attempts to the contrary, these elements of my legacy were thriving. Using a charitable organization to try to harm me was a dishonourable tactic and it reflected poorly on those who chose to do this. The only people who were really harmed were those who Espace and the organizations within it were seeking to support – the youth of our nation. Surely the people of Seychelles deserved better than this.

In the event, it was not politics which undermined the arrangement but the onset of the Covid-19 epidemic. Great damage was done to the economy in so many ways, not least of all in bankrupting the kind of small business which could find a home in Espace. Even if they were not forced into closure, confidence was damaged and investment decisions deferred. In the new business environment, Espace could no longer provide an assured revenue stream. Putting the property up for sale was a sad but inevitable end to an entirely worthy venture.

Because of the structure of governance, my position as Patron of the Jj Spirit Foundation precluded me from trying to force a different decision. A Board was in operation at Espace and it was the decision of that body which ended this particular chapter of events. I could only respect the right of the Board to do this, although for me it was a sad and probably needless outcome.

Reflection

To what purpose is this waste?[78]

'Look Back in Anger' was the title of a play written by John Osborne in the 1950s. But it is not with anger that I am looking back now. Nor with bitterness. Regret, perhaps, and sorrow, but most of all puzzlement. A once-familiar landscape that I had helped to create is no more. I look back and see so many elements of my legacy cast aside and I simply ask why. Was this new approach in the best interests of fellow Seychellois? Regrettably, it seems to be me as if, when I left the Office of the President, the clock was turned back and my legacy wilfully squandered. Many of the people I had appointed in various positions were cast aside for no obvious reason. It is not paranoia but reflection which leads me to wonder if some of the actions were motivated by anything more than a personal vendetta. It is a sad conclusion but let me say why I am left with these thoughts.

As I have already pointed out in an earlier section, it is only natural that a new leader will wish to make his or her own mark. I did so myself in my time. The electorate looks for new ideas and change, in the hope that these will take things forward. Faced with this prospect, on becoming president my successor might well have considered two options. He could either have wiped the slate clean, in the process removing me from any continuing influence; or he could have taken what was there and enriched it, perhaps asking me to strengthen his position within the party or play an ambassadorial role. In the event, he chose the former.

As an illustration of this, the most damaging reversal of events was surely the dismantling of what I had done to strengthen the security and reputation of the country. I put my name to the various initiatives, which were all in the national interest. To take the first of the related issues, drugs are a menace and the new measures I put in place were certainly making inroads in stalling the import of forbidden substances. The previous system was corrupt and I had no option but to remove responsibility from those who had abused it. So why did my successor abolish the NDEA in favour of returning responsibility to the police? I know that new personnel were brought in but the absence of a dedicated drug enforcement body can only be good news for organized crime.

As a result of this reversal, the interception record was reduced and heroin and other substances continued to flow into the country, causing immeasurable harm to our people. I accept that there was an emphasis on addiction treatment but that should have been as well as, not instead of, a tougher policy on preventing drug imports. There are at least 5000 users of heroin in Seychelles, equivalent to 10% of the working population (a much higher proportion if measured amongst young people), a situation that no economy with aspirations to be successful can afford. And the social repercussions in families and communities are profound, extending well beyond the number directly affected. One of the government's palliatives is methadone treatment but that reaches barely one third of addicts and is in any case a contentious remedy. White vans tour the districts each morning to dispense the product and the clusters of individuals queuing to receive their daily dose is not a sight to gladden the heart, nor to send tourists home with a favourable impression of paradise. It is a desperately sad business for all concerned and I am simply not convinced that enough was being done to stem the flow of drugs into the country in the first place.

REFLECTION

On a par with the haven that Seychelles provides for drug smugglers was the easing of restrictions on money laundering. The body that I set up to control the situation, the FIU, continued to operate. But, by all accounts, it was no longer the organization it was, enfeebled by the removal of regulations that I had introduced. As a result, there were no seizures of criminal proceeds resulting from money laundering after I stood down from office and, at the time of writing, during my successor's presidency not a single new case had been lodged in the courts. Worst of all, almost SCR 350 million of funds suspected of being the proceeds of crime and corruption, and which had been frozen by the courts and the FIU before the end of 2016, was released because of the new changes in money laundering laws. It is clear that the legal changes were deliberately designed to force the release of the seized funds from the independent arbitration of the Judiciary. I would like to see the transfers of this money investigated to identify those who benefited at the expense of law-abiding Seychellois. Confiscated cars and property were returned to traffickers and, instead of having their drug money passed to the state, people who should be branded as criminals have actually been paid compensation by the government.

Finally, the creation of a national intelligence system is yet another story of reversal. What earthly reason could there be for undoing the product of years of hard work that, by its very definition, was in the national interest? Everything was in place, awaiting government and parliamentary approval, only to be pared back at the eleventh hour. Yet threats remain on a number of fronts. Piracy has been effectively contained off the coast of Somalia but the source has not been removed. Fortunately, we have not been a target for terrorism but other countries in the region have and it would be folly to relax our guard. And smuggling is now rife in this part of the Indian Ocean, not only drugs but also other forms of contraband, and even human trafficking. Large container ships and traditional dhows alike, carrying illegal cargo, ply the waters seeking to exploit any lack of surveillance. Organized crime operates globally, looking for weak links where they will not be troubled. Without our own system of intelligence, criminals will be further encouraged to see Seychelles as a soft target for their unwanted activities. We have lowered our guard and will pay the price. Our reputation in the international community can only suffer.

Another national project that I pioneered is the Blue Economy. On the surface, it would seem that this remained a high-profile area of government activity, attracting international attention. Beneath the surface, however, I could see that there was an absence of leadership and good organization. First it was the responsibility of the vice-president, but his other duties were onerous and it was duly passed to the Foreign Secretary. The president delivered all the right words but was the passion to really make a difference still there? Where was a committed sense of direction? The fact is that I know the Blue Economy could be so much more. Seychelles had already made a name as a leading proponent of the idea and, from the outset, this was internationally recognized. A number of important initiatives were started and it is these which are now coming to fruition. But where are the new initiatives? It is not so much that what is being done is wrong, rather that the momentum was not being carried forward as it might have been. Surely, Seychelles was in pole position to find international partners willing to support a centre of excellence in Blue Economy research? And alongside this, perhaps, a centre for enterprise and innovation to integrate maritime research with the business community and our economy. We already had a head start but lost ground in the period from the end of 2016, having to witness our hard-won lead in this field slipping away to other nations with greater vision.

I had high hopes, too, for the University of Seychelles, where I remained Chancellor following my resignation as the nation's president. My vision was for our own university to play a leading role in the nation's journey to become a knowledge economy. UniSey was established in 2009 and good progress was made in the first seven years. But under the new regime the growth trajectory stalled. President Faure has been keen to sign agreements with foreign nations eager to allocate student places at their own universities. These are not reciprocal arrangements, so the effect has been to reduce the number of local students who might otherwise have helped to build our own institution. It is a one-way flow, without the advantage of international students coming to Seychelles. In spite of earlier promises of help, nothing has been done to provide residences for visiting students, nor (during that period) to make it easier to obtain visas and part-time work permits. It was also my wish that the Anse Royale campus would become the cultural centre of growth plans for the coastal township. The university itself could have been at the heart of bold plans to attract international visitors to festivals and other features of a lively venue. Although I remained Chancellor until early 2021, I was no longer informed of developments or invited to share in important decisions, and I fear for the future of what could so easily have become by now another jewel in the crown of Seychelles. It is only, now, with a new government, that I can see a positive move to strengthen the role of the nation's university.

In an earlier chapter, I spoke proudly of making the New Seychelles work but that is not what I could see continuing. It was as if the principles enshrined in the Constitution of the Third Republic were being systematically shredded. Not least of all, instead of a harmonious society composed of people of different races, xenophobia reared its ugly head and I could see no evidence of it being repelled. In debates in the National Assembly and in social media there was a negativity that can only sap the spirit of our nation. And, unforgivably, organized crime has been allowed to gain a new hold in our country. So many issues require decisive action that can only be achieved through strong leadership. But what I saw, instead, was inaction, reacting to rather than anticipating events. I could see the country calling in vain for decisions. It is little wonder that as I reflect on the past few years I feel disappointment, if not a sense of betrayal, that the legacy I passed on was so quickly and, in my view needlessly, cast aside. 'Where there is no vision the people perish' is a well-known biblical adage and, alas, it has become all too applicable in our own land.

Nothing, however, is for ever. As I write the final words of this book, the period in which my successor led the nation has come to an end. In the elections that were held towards the end of October 2020, power changed hands. The people could see that their interests were not best served. A new president was elected, no longer from the party that had ruled Seychelles since 1977, but from the main opposition party, Linyon Demokratik Seselwa (LDS). The reins of power are now in the hands of President Wavel Ramkalawan and the country is embarking on a new agenda.

It would be churlish to direct all of the blame for electoral defeat on Danny Faure as it was clear that the country was ready for a change. Forty-three years is a long time for one party to be in power and, in a democracy, it is not surprising that opinion swung in this way. What did take me by surprise was that, amongst some members of the ousted party, I was personally held responsible for the election outcome. Although small in number, they accused me of not giving my unequivocal backing for the campaign to re-elect Danny Faure. Not only that, but it was claimed that I had privately lent my support to the then opposition leader, Wavel Ramkalawan. There was a viciousness in the accusations that, in my view only served to discredit the accusers. It was clear that they wanted to deflect any blame from the defeated president and were not prepared to acknowledge some of the most obvious reasons for the convincing win of the opposition. Simply tarring me as a scapegoat was an easier option.

A dispassionate review of what went wrong would surely have been more constructive. An honest appraisal, for instance, might have looked more closely at the gap that had opened between the president and his party. In an attempt to demonstrate that he represented all of the people, perhaps he distanced himself too much from the party to which he had belonged.

Could he any longer count on the unequivocal support which I had previously enjoyed? Questions might also have been asked about Danny Faure's record in his four years as the country's leader. What had he actually done in that time, voters would have asked, to take things forward? Indeed, how will history mark his own legacy? There was, it seemed to me, a sense of lethargy about State House: the same ministers were still in office, there were obvious shortcomings in public service delivery, the drugs problem had not been addressed and, quite simply, there were no new ideas. It was as if the motor of government had run out of fuel. That was hardly a basis to win the hearts and minds of the electorate. And, to add to that, the opposition seemed to be offering something fresh.

It remains, however, for others to assess whether a different kind of leadership in the period since 2016 would have made a decisive difference. But to attempt to put the blame for the election result on me only shows just how far these disaffected party members were from the truth.

Part 3

A Glimpse of the Future

The future depends on what you do today.[79]

- ❖ **Recognition**
- ❖ **Agenda**
- ❖ **Utopia**

My Foundation provides a platform for continuing work on the Blue Economy, Sustainability and Climate Change

In this book I have, necessarily, looked back in an attempt to correct the record and rebut unwarranted criticism of my own leadership. But it is not in my nature to stand still. Since stepping down as president, I have already laid the basis for an active and fulfilling future. Through the James Michel Foundation, I am playing a fresh role in supporting a cause – the cause of our great seas, the cause of the Blue Economy – that means so much to me. It is heartening that there are now many other organizations across the world heading in the same direction too.

I have said farewell to the disappearing skyline of politics, where I spent so many years of my life, and it is with excitement rather than regret that I am now looking ahead. Optimism and hope drive me forward to meet challenges anew. I see hope in the eyes of my daughter, Laeticia, and I know that I cannot tire in my efforts. The future belongs to her and everyone else of her generation.

One advantage of being beyond the bounds of government is that I am free to follow my own instincts. Ideas no longer have to be filtered through a sieve of committees and the, sometimes emasculating, forces of compromise. Of course, reality still imposes its own constraints – there is no point in coming up with ideas that stand no chance of adoption – but the scope to be inventive is undoubtedly greater than before. It is a luxury that I do not intend to squander. There is another advantage, too, in not being constrained by any one jurisdiction and that is my opportunity to work internationally, where my ideas and record are widely acknowledged. I love my country deeply but I love the world too. And the words of a seventeenth-century French expression (with biblical origins) rings true in my own mind: *nul n'est prophète dans son pays*. One is sometimes better appreciated abroad than at home.

'The future depends on what you do today', said the inspirational Mahatma Gandhi, and today can indeed be regarded as the starting point for the next phase in my own life. The last few years have had their challenges but those are now behind me. Although in relation to the future of our connected seas the obstacles we face are formidable, the sheer volume of support in favour of change is overwhelming. The inter-related concepts of the Blue Economy, Sustainability, and Climate Change, that are at the heart of my own Foundation, are now part of the international currency of global conservation. These are now everyday terms and our understanding of them increases by the day. Digital transformation has made these vital issues everyone's business. Once the domain only of scientists and other specialists, or seen as being restricted to limited geographical areas, an awareness of these subjects has become ubiquitous. They are global in scope. The challenge belongs to us all, as does the future.

In this final chapter I want to focus again on what I can do personally, and through my own organization, to achieve my aims. I believe that the values embodied in my legacy can still inform what lies ahead. It retains its worth and Gandhi's words about the future starting now are certainly not lost. We can build on what has already been done; a better future is surely within our collective reach.

Recognition

We are members one of another.[80]

In preparing to take the first steps into the future, it helps that what I have done before has been generously acknowledged by prestigious organizations and individuals across the world. If, as it would seem, my contribution is not presently required in official circles at home, at least there is no shortage of opportunities overseas. Seychelles is part of a global community and we are, indeed, members 'one of another'. It reflects well on my country as well as myself that I am part of an international network, in which I enjoy not only recognition but also the chance to be actively involved with like-minded campaigners. To illustrate the extent and calibre of this network, I can point to some of the most recent appointments and awards that I have received.

- Following the climate change agreement in Paris in 2015 and the adoption of the UN's Sustainable Development Goals, the World Sustainable Development Forum was created to provide grassroots impetus for their full implementation. In recognition of my proven commitment to the cause, I was appointed as a Patron of this organization.

- In 2017, I was invited to serve as a member of the Advisory Board of the Group on Earth Observations Oceans and Society: Blue Planet Initiative (GEO Blue Planet).

- In that same year, I was recognized as an Ocean's 8 Champion by the Intergovernmental Oceanographic Commission of

UNESCO at the UN Ocean conference in New York, for developing our innovative debt swap scheme to enable funding for local ocean science and climate resilience programmes in Seychelles.

As an Ocean Ambassador, with fellow members (Dona Bertarelli, John Kerry and Heraldo Muñoz) of the Pew Bertarelli Ocean Legacy Project

♦ In 2018, I was invited to be a founding member of the Pew Bertarelli Ocean Ambassadors. This is a small group of global leaders who work with the Pew Bertarelli Ocean Legacy Project to advocate the creation of large marine protected areas. Co-chaired by John Kerry and David Cameron, in association with Dona Bertarelli, I am one of just five Ocean Ambassadors. We will play our part in securing an increase in the number of marine protected areas, as a contribution towards the protection, in this way, of 30% of the world's oceans by 2030.

- Then, in April 2019, I received an invitation to join the exclusive World Leadership Alliance Club de Madrid. This organization is the world's largest forum of democratically elected former presidents and prime ministers, with members from more than seventy countries. It was a particular source of pride that my candidacy was actively supported by two former presidents, Cassam Uteem of Mauritius and Bill Clinton of the United States, as well as the former Secretary-General of the United Nations, Ban Ki-moon.

Members are committed to sharing their experience in government and to overcoming the challenges of leadership in contemporary politics worldwide. The Club de Madrid advocates for a 'democracy that delivers' and works in partnership with other organizations and governments which share its objectives. The Club also works with a broad network of international experts and practitioners, towards addressing issues of global concern such as intolerance, violent extremism, climate change and social cohesion from a democratic perspective.

- Just two months later, I made my way to Washington DC to receive a much-prized Planetary Leadership Award from National Geographic to mark my contribution to ocean sustainability. National Geographic is an outstanding body that I have long admired and I feel greatly honoured to be recognized in this way. As I remarked in my acceptance speech, the legendary author and campaigner, Rachel Carson, reminded us many years ago that human evolution started in the sea. Yet that is where survival is now most threatened. Not only for humans but other living creatures too. We cannot allow the loss of a single species.

I went on to say that National Geographic does wonderful work and I intend to continue to do everything I can to support its mission, the ultimate vision of which is 'a planet in balance'. In a closing clarion call I urged that:

> *Now is the time for our reconciliation with the oceans! Now is the time to strike a balance between our needs and the conservation and rehabilitation of our oceans! With a new compass, we could chart the journey for the future. There is only one message: Healing, Conservation and Sustainability. Our shared future is Blue.*

Receiving a Planetary Leadership Award to mark my contribution to ocean sustainability. At the ceremony it was a great honour to renew my acquaintance with the great explorer of the ocean, Sylvia Earle

- Following my visit to Washington, I was then invited to join the International Advisory Panel of Australia's prestigious

Oceanic Research Institute. With its three missions of education, communication and research, I was well placed to make a valuable contribution.

♦ In addition to the above memberships and awards, I am regularly invited to speak at international conferences. In responding to these invitations, I am selective in what I attend but I maintain a presence wherever I think it would be most beneficial. One such event where I thought this would be the case was the World Ocean Summit held in Abu Dhabi in March 2019 (alluded to in the previous chapter). Unfortunately, with the funeral of the late President René in that same week I was unable to attend in person. Instead, I sent the following message in the form of a video. I am including it below as it was well received and illustrates what I believe to be important priorities in this field.

> *In the short time available I will make three practical observations on the ocean, based on what we have already learnt in our quest to make the land of our precious planet more sustainable. In this respect, blue follows green; now we need the two to advance together.*
>
> ***First, we must plan the use of the ocean.*** *We should build on the experience of land-use planning to create a similar process for the sea. It is almost inconceivable that most of the world's seas are still something of a 'free for all'. As well as the high seas, many of the areas under national jurisdiction remain little more than lines on a map. We must now zone sections for different uses and support the UN's work to bring the high seas under control.*
>
> *In my own small island state of Seychelles we are presently*

preparing a plan to match our ocean responsibilities. It is time for all countries to do this and to create a maritime planning system with a new generation of ocean planners.

Second, we need to work with businesses and communities. *This is another lesson from land-use planning. Governments are good at guiding and encouraging. But (as I am sure this conference will show) it is businesses which will see the opportunities to innovate and invest. And it is communities which can give energy and local know-how to make plans work. The best plans are not imposed from above but they grow from within. Plans are nourished by people. Success can only be achieved through ownership!*

Finally, we need some quick wins. *Simply talking will not save the ocean. People now accept land-use planning because it can offer examples like national parks and sustainable neighbourhoods. I believe that at sea the real eye-catcher is marine protected areas. These can really make a dramatic difference and my own small nation is committed to making its own contribution. Marine protected areas are not difficult to establish so long as there is political will. If the world as a whole can reach the target of 30% protection we will have marked a famous victory. We still have a long way to go but we can do it.*

From time to time, I receive new awards and other tokens of recognition for my work

❖
Agenda

The new normal will not be any normal we know. It is a complete global reboot of our existing way of life and organization, everything involved in purpose, process, work location, and local variations.[81]

Has there ever been a time more in need of fresh ideas? Planet Earth is in poor shape. Mostly, this is because humans have treated it so badly. The gravity of the situation is measured by the fact that there is no one factor responsible for what can only be seen as a global crisis. Instead, a combination of circumstances has together brought us to the present situation. Yet, one must ask, as the problems are largely made by humans, how we have allowed this to happen? It is not as if there was no warning of what was to come. For those who took the trouble to look around them, the signs were ominous. Storm clouds have been gathering over a long period, urging us to take note. Even when they first appeared, they already showed the potential to bring havoc to the world. But we largely ignored what was there to see, carrying on with our lives regardless. Our indifference is proving to be more costly than we could possibly have imagined. It is as if we were prepared to sleepwalk into oblivion.

In the event, it has taken a pandemic to rudely awaken us. Global systems of trade and communication, which we had taken for granted, were by no means as robust as we had assumed. Indeed, the whole idea of globalization came into question. Our thinking had become lazy. We were deluding ourselves. It suited us to believe there would always be more food on the table than previous generations had known; we could travel, at the drop of a credit card, from one part of the world to another; everyone aspired to a western lifestyle and ways would be found to deliver it. Cheap clothes from low-wage countries; exotic fruits throughout the year; holidays when we wanted; homes full of gadgets. The long history of human progress had led us to a utopian land of plenty. Nothing was allowed to spoil our delusions. Of course, there would be problems, but these could be resolved. Burgeoning cities, for instance, generated mountains of waste every day but, never mind, new technologies would find a way to deal with it. Just as we could rely on solutions to endemic problems of traffic congestion, air pollution and poor housing, to name just a few. Great minds had come to our rescue before and there was no reason to doubt that they would do so again. Even while the clouds amassed overhead, life went on as normal. For most of the past decade (and, if we are honest, well before that), complacency and self-interest ruled the day. We were hooked on the idea of uninterrupted progress.

Coming to Terms

With hindsight, it is easy to see what was ignored. The threats to our future are surely clear enough and all are in need of a suitable response. Together they pose an enormous challenge and I would like to see my own Foundation serving as a think tank for what are clearly global issues. The agenda is formidable, a list of challenges, any one of which is daunting but which together might at first seem overwhelming. If we are to stand any chance of survival, I believe that there are six questions which demand urgent answers:

- **The world's climate is changing. So what?**

- **Will there be enough to eat?**

- **Should we regard pandemics as part of the 'new normal'?**

> - **What have we done to Mother Nature?**
>
> - **Are there just too many people on the planet?**
>
> - **Can we manage to live in peace with each other?**

The world's climate is changing. So what?

For a start, there is climate change, roughly brushed aside by the global panic over Covid-19 but requiring urgent attention more than ever.

> *Climate Change is the defining issue of our time and we are at a defining moment. From shifting weather patterns that threaten food production, to rising sea levels that increase the risk of catastrophic flooding, the impacts of climate change are global in scope and unprecedented in scale. Without drastic action today, adapting to these impacts in the future will be more difficult and costly.*[82]

Like many other leaders – but certainly not all – I could see, at an early stage, the potential of climate change as a major threat to life as we know it. Scientists had been tracking the trend before that but it was in the new millennium that the issue started to make headlines. Before long, brought to everyone's attention by unprecedented natural events and news coverage, everyone was talking about it. And a broad consensus soon evolved, calling for answers. How should the inter-related problems be addressed?

If words and promises alone were enough to check the advance of climate change, we would be well on the way to managing the situation. There are few countries which have not spoken up on the subject and, even in a case like the United States, where the former president saw it in his own, idiosyncratic way, American citizens largely agreed with the rest of the world. 'Climate deniers', as they are called, are in a minority. Academic research papers, NGO statements, national declarations and numerous pronouncements by the United Nations, have all warned that action must be taken. When the UN, in Paris in 2015, voted in favour of measures to curb the rate of change, it marked something of a breakthrough in international cooperation. It was a cause for celebration and I am proud that I was still president when my own nation signed up to this historic agreement. But, as the saying goes, the devil is in the detail and, while many nations have since shown a real commitment to the cause, it is by no means universal. As a result, restraints on the rate of climate change are by no means as effective as intended. Across the world, there is urgent work still to be done, and different nations and the many organizations within them can each play an essential role.

Will there be enough to eat?

A second area of global concern, although not presently given the priority it deserves, is food security; an issue that will become ever more acute. As with climate change, we have been taking too much for granted, lulled into a false sense of security by the relative ease of buying food. It has become all too much of a routine to make one's way to local markets and stores – or, increasingly, ordering online for a delivery to the door – confident in the knowledge that there will be sufficient available. And with such choice. For the most developed parts of the world in modern times, that has become the case. But the good fortune of the majority overshadows the fate of millions more who, every day, go hungry or at best have to manage with a diet that is lacking in nutrition. We have forgotten that this kind of situation was not so long ago the norm, when finding ways to keep one's family alive and well was a daily challenge. We have forgotten, too, the frequent (and remarkably recent) incidence of famines, from which, for whole communities and sometimes entire countries, there was no escape.

In 2020, the global pandemic provided a sharp reminder that regular food supplies cannot be taken for granted. The cancellation of international flights and the closing of borders seriously disrupted both imports and exports, leaving communities in different parts of the world without regular supplies of food. And, beyond these specific circumstances, there is a bigger crisis looming. I have for long been concerned that the combination of more people in the world, combined with a diminishing supply of land, represents a balance that cannot be sustained. At the start of the nineteenth century the total population on earth stood at around 1 billion. By the middle of the twentieth century it had reached 2.5 billion. From that point, the rate of increase accelerated, so much so that by the turn of the millennium the world total had passed the 6 billion mark. And it will go on rising until it is expected to stabilize towards the end of the present century around the 10-11 billion mark.[83]

At the same time that numbers of people are increasing, there is less land to devote to farming. Year on year, large tracts of farmland are displaced by the relentless spread of burgeoning cities. And this is quite apart from the additional loss of growing areas as a result of soil erosion through bad farming practices; according to one report, over the past forty years this avoidable loss is equivalent to a third of the world's arable land.[84] Climate change is also playing its part, as a result, for instance, of rising sea levels leading to the encroachment of coastal land and, in other parts of the world, there is desertification. One way and another, the area available to produce food is, quite dramatically, diminishing.

Against this backcloth, should we be worried? I believe we should and, as a result, I find it surprising that the warning calls are not louder. There is work to be done and the issue is another one which I would like to see addressed by my own Foundation.

Should we regard pandemics as part of the new normal?

Thirdly, as the recent pandemic has shown, the potential for further instances of the global spread of disease must now be acknowledged as a continuing threat to human existence. The world was taken by surprise by the spread of Covid-19 but that was because earlier warnings had not been heeded. Just as was the case with climate change and food security, it was not that potential problems were unknown, it was simply that no-one was listening. During the 1990s, scientists were already showing why the chances of pandemics were increasing:

> *Experts were identifying conditions that could lead to the introduction of new, potentially devastating pathogens – climate change, massive urbanization, the proximity of humans to farm or forest animals that serve as viral reservoirs – with the worldwide spread of those microbes accelerated by war, the global economy, and international air travel.*[85]

Nor were such warnings merely abstract. Even before the ongoing pandemic, we experienced the spread of other viruses, with the potential to cause multiple fatalities. SARS, MERS, Ebola and swine flu were all to make their mark and showed the importance of being prepared, even to the extent of the common-sense precaution of stocking up on protective equipment for health workers. When he was President of the United States, Barack Obama warned his country of the need to be prepared for future outbreaks and he urged his fellow politicians to allocate a budget for the necessary actions. In a speech in December 2014, he explained:

> *There may and likely will come a time in which we have an airborne disease that is deadly, and in order for us to deal with that effectively we have to put in place an infrastructure, not just here at home but globally, that allows us to see it quickly, isolate it quickly, respond to it quickly...*[86]

His request was turned down and, little more than five years later, America found itself in the eye of a new storm. Such is the American system of checks and balances that, even if the incoming president, Donald Trump, had wanted to, he would have found it immensely difficult to persuade the governors of the different states to act in unison. As a result, the initial response to the latest pandemic could not be counted as America's finest hour, with more than eight million reported cases, of which the highest proportion of deaths occurred in the densely populated states of New York and New Jersey.[87]

At the time of writing, it is still too early to reflect accurately on the full impact of Covid-19. On the one hand, there has generally been a good recovery rate amongst patients, greatly improved when effective vaccinations came onto the market. And although, in absolute terms, the actual number of individuals around the world who contracted the virus was high, the proportion of the total population who died as a result is quite small and is usually accounted for by pre-existing health conditions. It remains to be seen whether governments over-reacted in their various forms of response, or whether they did what was right. One thing, however, is clear, Covid 19 has provided a dramatic wake-up call in alerting the world to the threat of pandemics. Next time (and there surely will be a next time) the strain of virus may prove to be more deadly and it would be irresponsible to ignore the lessons of the present one. To be forewarned is to be forearmed.

What have we done to Mother Nature?

Next, in spite of repeated warnings, there is the wanton treatment of our environment, both on land and at sea, and the threats to our future welfare that this brings. As early as the first century after the death of Christ, there was a sense that humans were being punished for their behaviour. Confronted with the volcanic eruption of Mount Vesuvius, the writer, Robert Harris, constructs the words of a contemporary observer, Pliny the

Elder, to convey feelings at the time:

> *Mother Nature is punishing us for our greed and selfishness. We torture her at all hours by iron and wood, fire and stone. We dig her up and dump her in the sea. We sink mine shafts into her and drag out her entrails – and all for a jewel to wear on pretty finery. Who can blame her if she occasionally quivers with anger?*[88]

Even allowing for the intervention of fiction, this kind of reaction to the historic event is perfectly plausible. Fire bursting from the earth, unprecedented in its impact, would, understandably, invite an expectation of deserved punishment by a greater power. At moments like that, it is more than likely that the price of human folly and an inner cry for forgiveness will dominate one's last thoughts. Pliny was, for his day, highly educated (with the world's first encyclopaedia to his name) and knew only too well what harm his fellow beings had already done to Mother Nature. It was his knowledge of this, and his natural curiosity, which drew him ever closer to the fearful scenes on the slopes of Vesuvius, until the sulphurous smoke led to his own suffocation.

Alas, such warnings proved in vain and every generation has added its own chapter to the cumulative tale of woe. No matter how we may now regard the rights and wrongs of human nature, and conjecture whether things could have turned out differently, the fact remains that the world's environment today is in a sorry state. On land and at sea, the situation is dire. In a recent report, just one amongst many, the United Nations warned that we were already at the cliff's edge:

> *2019 was a year when our past finally caught up with us and science provided an unambiguous call for urgent action. A year when the world witnessed devastating storms, ice sheets melting in the Arctic, giant wildfires and deadly floods. A year when we were warned that 1 million plant and animal species face extinction. A*

year when we were reminded that unless we act immediately to cut greenhouse gas emissions, we will alter life on earth forever.[89]

Yet, lemming-like, we continue to rush ahead. In spite of the best efforts of environmentalists, even the clearest of warnings are not heeded. If there is any comfort to be found, it is that people across the world are now more aware of what is happening and what is at stake. As a contribution to this largely spontaneous response, I would like to see my own Foundation show how much more can be done in Seychelles. Although this small nation enjoys a high level of protection, the sheer scale and intensity of modern development puts this at risk. The unique contribution that can be made will locate this process alongside the other threats, such as climate change and food security.

Are there just too many people on the planet?

There is a simplicity in the argument that more people on the planet makes human survival more difficult: requiring additional land when a rising sea level will reduce what is already there, putting further pressure on farmers to supply extra food, increasing the chances of future pandemics which thrive in high densities. And the argument is by no means new, as the following piece from a publication in the 1950s illustrates:

> *People are recognizing that we cannot forever continue to multiply and subdue the earth without losing our standard of life and the natural beauty that must be part of it. These are the years of decision...*[90]

World population would continue to rise, was the message, but only at a cost. Yet, since then, the number of people on the planet has grown exponentially and the warning has been cast aside. An opposing view has taken its place, asserting that science will come to our rescue, just as it has done before. I remain one of those who is not convinced.

As the former leader of a country that is part of Africa, I am acutely aware of why people are resentful of claims about overpopulation. People across this continent do not have more children for the sake of it but as a result of a combination of factors, including cultural traditions, economic necessity to bring into a family another pair of hands, and the simple fact that effective methods of birth control are often lacking. These people should not automatically be blamed for bringing more children into the world but, rather, through education and infrastructure, they can be helped to slow the birth rate.

While I understand the plight of fellow Africans, I can also see that it is those same people who will suffer most if numbers continue to grow at the present rate. In this impoverished continent, the present population will double to 2.4 billion by mid-century (equivalent to an increase of 42 million per year).[91] Against earlier expectations, the rate of reproduction has shown no signs of reducing; women in Niger, for instance, a country in a harsh environment on the edge of the Sahara, with a GDP per capita below US$ 1 per day, currently have more than seven children in their lifetime. Nigeria, a much larger country but with enormous problems of its own, is expected to exceed the population of the US within the next three decades. It is not only the scale of these increases but also the speed with which it is happening that gives cause for alarm. Over a longer period, there might just be opportunities to make adjustments; at the present rate, taking a measured approach is not an option.

One way and another the issue of population growth is inseparable from the other major problems facing the world, and it is one that needs more urgent attention than it has so far attracted.

Can we manage to live in peace with each other?

Finally, there is the one issue which transcends all others, that of whether we can manage to live in peace with each other. Unless we can do that, in the nuclear age nothing else will matter. Unfortunately, the record of living peaceably is not good. People, whether in tribes or nations, have too readily taken to arms to resolve disputes. Wars are as old as human history. For those who engage in combat, and for civilians on the sidelines, the immediacy of death and destruction is like a guillotine waiting to fall. This has always been the case. But for most of history, wars have been localized. What is different now is the question of scale, with conflict potentially involving the entire human race. Towards the very end of the Second World War, the advent of nuclear weapons, with the capacity to destroy the whole of the earth and its people, changed the entire terms of engagement. The clouds that warn of global warfare have darkened the skies since 1945. Of all the warnings about the future, because of its threat of finality, this is the most chilling.

In spite of the enormity of the threat, as with the other issues on the global agenda, is there any evidence that we have taken heed? Are we prepared to act to prevent Armageddon? Certainly, strategies have been devised to stave off outright war. But these are by no means foolproof and have to take account of the idiosyncrasies of human nature, as well as the intrigues and uncertainties of international power politics. In spite of the dire warnings that global warfare must be avoided at all costs, there is still abundant evidence that the world is not listening.

When the Cold War ended, with the removal of the Berlin Wall and the subsequent dissolution of the Soviet Union, tensions were reduced and, in the euphoria surrounding the transition, the world could breathe a sigh of relief. But it was soon apparent that the nuclear threat had not disappeared too. The newly-formed state of Russia inherited the bulk of the former USSR's nuclear stock but not all of the weapons were accounted for, giving rise to the possibility of nuclear-armed terrorists and the possession of nuclear warheads by rogue states. Moreover, with North Korea flexing its muscles and Iran trying to develop its own capacity, there was even less chance of controlling the situation. To add to it all, the economic ascendancy of China and its sharpening rivalry with the US introduced a new dimension. Small states like my own supported moves for non-proliferation but were otherwise unable to determine events that affected us all. It was not that we ignored the threat to the planet that was there for all to see, but we were marginalized by the great powers. We could see the dangers of the situation but could only hope that reason and good sense would prevail.

Yet this is one of those instances where hope is not enough. History shows that humans cannot be trusted not to go to war, in which case there have to be other mechanisms to uphold peace. There have to be international rules and the capacity and will of nations to uphold them. Finding ways to achieve this, I believe, is the greatest challenge of all. But it can certainly not be ignored and I would want to see it on the same agenda as the other issues listed in this section.

A Tiny Blue Dot

To put all this into perspective, I can do no better than to quote the words of the astronomer, Carl Sagan, who reflected on the iconic photograph of the earth from space in which we appear as no more than a tiny blue dot:

> *The Earth is a very small stage in a vast cosmic arena. Think of the rivers of blood spilled by all those generals and emperors so that, in glory and triumph, they could become the momentary masters of a fraction of a dot. Think of the endless cruelties visited by the inhabitants of one corner of this pixel on the scarcely distinguishable inhabitants of some other corner, how frequent their misunderstandings, how eager they are to kill one another, how fervent their hatreds.*

Our posturings, our imagined self-importance, the delusion that we have some privileged position in the Universe, are challenged by this point of pale light. Our planet is a lonely speck in the great enveloping cosmic dark. In our obscurity, in all this vastness, there is no hint that help will come from elsewhere to save us from ourselves.

The Earth is the only world known so far to harbor life. There is nowhere else, at least in the near future, to which our species could migrate. Visit, yes. Settle, not yet. Like it or not, for the moment the Earth is where we make our stand.

It has been said that astronomy is a humbling and character-building experience. There is perhaps no better demonstration of the folly of human conceits than this distant image of our tiny world. To me, it underscores our responsibility to deal more kindly with one another, and to preserve and cherish the pale blue dot, the only home we've ever known.[92]

Utopia

Not in Utopia – subterranean fields –
Or some secreted island, Heaven knows where!
But in the very world, which is the world
Of all of us – the place where, in the end
We find our happiness, or not at all![93]

Let us end on an upbeat note, focusing not on those many views which are based on doom and gloom but, instead, on hope. In the face of adversity, an alternative vision can be presented of a world where wrongs are put to right. We can allow ourselves to think of a better future, maybe not just better but perfect. Such is the vision of utopia.

Against a backcloth of global crisis in its many forms, turning the pages of utopian texts is a refreshing experience. The idea of perfection is seductive. We are so used to imagining the worst, that confronting the best is not only therapeutic but also intellectually stimulating. A world where people live in peace, where there is enough for all to satisfy their needs, where cooperation is at the heart of everything, where there is no crime, no need for prisons; a world where forests flourish and the seas are once again pristine. And we soon find that this search for perfection is not a momentary experience but a longstanding human impulse. The Garden of Eden, for instance, was an early example of untainted harmony, an ideal construct in one form or another that was by no means confined to the Judaeo-Christian tradition nor, indeed, just to the distant past. From one generation to another, different versions of a Golden Age have surfaced. Thus, in the sixteenth century, Thomas More, with his fictional island, Utopia, gave the name to the whole genre and encouraged those who followed him to engage on their own quests for perfection. Explorers crossed the seven seas, believing that discovery of a previously unknown island would reveal a hidden paradise. Some writers suggested, instead, that this wondrous place could only be found beneath the earth or amongst the stars. Under the various banners of religion and socialism, spirituality and anarchism, utopians have continued to follow a well-worn path, a repeated reminder for humanity that the world need not be as it is.

But the story of utopia, though full of hope, is also tinged with sadness as, time and again, such journeys lead nowhere. The faraway horizon is crossed but only to reveal that there is nothing beyond. Like a mirage, the golden vision dissolves before one's eyes. In the wake of so many disappointments, surely the conclusion is that it has all been a wasted effort. The record tells its own story.

Or is there something more at stake, perhaps a recognition that, while perfection itself is beyond reach, a better world is still possible. Although utopians discovered that the road they followed with such high hopes, in fact, led nowhere, surely all was not lost? Was it still possible to salvage some of their goals to improve the world around them? The outcome might not be perfect, in the sense they had hoped for, but it could still make society better than it was. Perhaps an element of realism is not to be dismissed. Even a romantic poet like William Wordsworth, who in so many ways put his faith in imagination and decried the cold logic of rationality, rightly pointed out that if happiness is to be found anywhere it can only be in the real world. Published after the poet's death, the lines at the start of this section put a lie to the eternal quest for utopia as a place which remains obstinately no more than a dream. Why not look instead at the here and now?

So let us learn from the past. It would be folly to ignore the multitude of failures and to believe that there is still an undiscovered path leading to absolute perfection, let alone the existence of a 'secreted island'. We might well harbour thoughts of utopia but is it not better to exchange a vision that is illusory for a world that retains some blemishes but also great improvements? Is it really misguided to seek a better, albeit still imperfect, world? Do we have to accept, for instance, that our seas must remain so heavily polluted when it is within our means to remove much of the waste? Is it really so strange to want to pass on to future generations a planet that is fit to live in, with many of the riches that nature can offer? And, while there are aspects of climate change that cannot be stopped, some can indeed be checked if not reversed; so why are we not doing more to achieve this?

If there is to be progress across the world, then at some point there must be international agreements. But these often result from the exemplary actions of individual nations, which might show in practice how meaningful improvements can be attained. Such actions are not necessarily the product of major powers but, equally, can be initiated within small states. Bhutan is a good example, a landlocked nation in the eastern Himalayas, which has gone out of its way to maintain its integrity, cultural as well as environmental. But it is probably best known for spreading the idea of measuring development in terms of Gross National Happiness (GNH) instead of Gross National Product (GNP).[94]

> *The concept implies that sustainable development should take a holistic approach towards notions of progress and give equal importance to non-economic aspects of wellbeing… The GNH Index includes both traditional areas of socio-economic concern such as living standards, health and education and less traditional aspects of culture and psychological wellbeing. It is a holistic reflection of the general wellbeing of the Bhutanese population rather than a subjective psychological ranking of 'happiness' alone.*[95]

Bhutan has, quite dramatically, challenged conventional wisdom and caused the rest of the world to take note. I believe that Seychelles can do the same, not by replicating landlocked Bhutan but through demonstrating our own novel ideas that reflect our oceanic location and the particular challenges we face. We have already shown ourselves to be innovative in many ways and, if the will is there, we can continue to set an example. Somewhere on this side of utopia there is endless scope for ideas and innovation.

So, within the familiar shores of Seychelles and in the surrounding sea, what new ideas can we offer to the rest of the world? There is already a great deal in the pipeline, much of which dates back to the time when I was president. The contribution of this legacy is not to be underestimated but still more needs to be done. Seychelles could become an acknowledged hub for ocean recovery, a place where ideas lead to action.

We should, perhaps, invite some of the best minds in the world to spend time on our islands, sharing their own thoughts and creating new ones. I am not thinking of a conventional conference so much as an opportunity to get people together in an informal setting and to see what emerges. And that would be only the first step, with a common objective being to create a permanent legacy. In our own way we could create the Silicon Valley of the Indian Ocean. There is no limit to ideas that can make a real difference. To take just a few:

- A problem which all small island states face, Seychelles included, is to prevent the illegal use of their ocean space by other nations. The technology is now available through drones and satellite surveillance to monitor and prevent this but the financial costs of doing so inhibit progress. I would dearly love to see our own precious seas protected in this way, using new technologies to the full for the benefit of all. Through a demonstration project of this sort, it would be possible not only to extend such systems to other jurisdictions but also to enable the proper management of the high seas.

- We need to promote more widely the value of reserving, as we are currently doing, 30% of the sea within our jurisdiction as protected space. It will include areas where there should be no fishing at all and other parts where it is carefully managed, to allow stocks to recover and, more widely, an embargo on deep-sea mining. This will ensure sustainability for future generations and sets an example which we hope other nations will adopt. If, in time, this 30% target can be applied to all of the world's oceans, including the high seas, it will mark a momentous transformation for the world.

- As a more specific project, why not, more generally, a 'one-stop' global shop window for good ideas and practical projects that will further the cause of the Blue Economy? Just as we now see a proliferation of online websites for consumers, individual states need good and accessible advice on what is effective and what is reliable. This is a simple and achievable target, where the basic software already exists. If it works when an individual wants to buy a car, why not for states wanting to invest in renewable energy? In the global shop window, one could see at a glance where the best examples of good practice are located, and how the limits of sustainable energy are constantly being pushed back. In relation to what it could yield, it would be a very cost-effective project, requiring a relatively small team of bright IT personnel and a base for their work. This is something which could easily be accommodated in the capital of Seychelles or, alternatively, at the nation's university, with the sound of the sea a constant spur to innovation.

- Why not, too, the development of an international network of centres of excellence, furthering the cause of one specific activity in each case. Given my belief that small island states are well placed to work on the frontline of ocean research, they might well take a lead. To offer some examples, Seychelles could be the home of progressive Blue Economy management schemes; Samoa, say, could offer to the world working examples of ocean waste management; Cape Verde could be the centre for tidal energy – and so on. The idea is that the enormous challenge of making better use of the ocean can be broken down into manageable, 'bite-sized' chunks, each of which is within the capability of individual states. And with the added attraction that the rest of us will know where to go for advice and demonstration activities.

- A further example of what might be done is, ideally through the UN, for every coastal nation to complete a survey of their own shoreline, including harbours and redundant buildings, to see how these might be better used. There is already a substantial infrastructure in place but is it being used to its full potential? At the interface of the green and blue economies, these areas have a pivotal role. Apart from anything else, this could involve young and old in carrying out local surveys and offering ideas based on their own experience. I would especially like to see schools and places of higher learning as part of this process. And we could add, to this, competitions for coastal architecture to ensure that everything about the sea is of the highest quality.

- There is no doubt, too, that we should generate ideas to bring more women into the maritime workforce. It has been estimated by the International Transport Workers' Federation that only 2% of the world's maritime workforce is presently made up of women. Can we really afford to exclude nearly half of the population from an exercise that should involve us all? Changing the balance would not simply add to the number of ideas but it would undoubtedly encourage new perceptions too.

- Let us, as well, invite the UN to design and fund a programme of annual awards for the most important contributions to the sustainable use of our shared ocean. This would encourage competition and highlight some of the excellent work that is already underway across the world. The whole emphasis would be on practical achievements.

It is time to give our imagination free rein. I can envisage a future when our coastal communities host a new form of active tourism, with festivals to celebrate aspects of our environment. I can envisage markets selling sustainable products from the sea, including food harvested from the subterranean plant life. And I can envisage renewable energy from the ocean's currents and waves, on a scale that is not yet possible but surely will be before long. This is not a time to be defeatist. The ocean is our future and we should do everything we can to respond to what is on offer.

Even beyond the ocean, our common mission is surely to create a planet in balance – capable of reproducing itself so that future generations can live in harmony with nature and with each other. I have urged elsewhere that it is the responsibility of every political leader in the world to work towards the preservation of our ecosystem, the preservation of the ocean, preservation of the land, and preservation of the planet.[96]

I can see Seychelles itself as a real game-changer, a place of inspiration in our global community. Or, in the words of the seventeenth-century poet, John Dryden, *Fairest isle, all isles excelling...*[97] Fairest isle, indeed. Is there a better note on which to end, or on which to begin?

210 PART 3 - A GLIMPSE OF THE FUTURE

Optimism must be nourished, the sea is our future

Epilogue

Time present and time past
Are both perhaps present in time future,
And time future contained in time past.[98]

An epilogue will usually signify the end of a story. In part, this is what this final page does. It allows me to reaffirm that I wrote this book to fill a gap in the modern history of Seychelles, and to set the record straight. I have been able to explain the making of my legacy and to recount how it was subsequently received. Allegations have been made about some of my actions and in the preceding pages I have been able to rebut these. In telling the truth I have called to mind an African proverb which claims that 'he who tells the truth is never wrong'. My conscience is clear. I have said what I wanted. It is now time to move on.

But this was never just about me. I have taken what I believe is undeserved criticism. But my belief in democracy is undiminished. Although it is not a perfect system it is the best we have. It gives people a say in how we live. In the course of my presidency, everything I did was for the good of Seychelles. Reforms were put in place and real improvements followed. More than that, I never lost sight of the values that make our country so special. If I find myself now with a sense of disappointment, it is not at a personal level. Instead, my regret is that some of my measures were reversed and one must question why. And it is as if the values we espouse were left to wither on the vine. To recover lost ground, I believe that a fresh political impetus is needed. There has been too much negativity and too little hope. It is surely time for this to change. In the interests of the country we all love, I wish the new leader of Seychelles well. As I do for those who follow him too.

And so the story is unfinished. There is more work to be done and we look not only to politicians but also to active citizens across our islands to take a lead. We are blessed to live in such a favoured part of the world. Although today there are storm clouds overhead, we know they will pass. It will not be like this forever. Optimism will return and with it a new agenda for a bright future, one that is rooted in the sound Creole values that are imbued in our culture. We can learn from the past but we must never be trapped in it. Now we need to move forward. We owe it to ourselves and to generations to come.

The end of one story is the beginning of another. This is an epilogue but also a prologue.

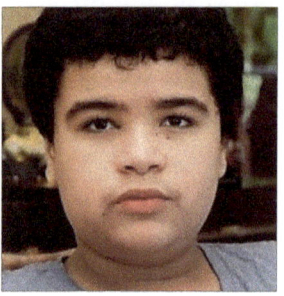

The end of one story is the beginning of another. My son, Jean-Claude, with my daughter, Laeticia; and my two grandsons, Jude (top right) and Dylan (bottom right)

Notes and References

1. William Shakespeare, *All's Well That Ends Well*, Act III, Scene V.
2. *Corinthians,* 13:12, King James Version.
3. Composite dictionary definition.
4. D.H. Lawrence, 'The Man Who Loved Islands'. In Patrick Barham (2017). *Islander: A Journey Around Our Archipelago.* London: Granta, p.52.
5. H.G. Wells (1895). *The Time Machine*, Chapter 1: Introduction. First published as a book by William Heinemann, London.
6. James Michel (2011). *Distant Horizons: My Reflections.* London: Rila Publications.
7. *Ibid*, p.9.
8. Colonial Office (1948). *Annual Report on Seychelles for the Year 1946.* London: HMSO, p.2.
9. The official number of volunteers who fought with the Allies is 1730.
10. Colonial Office, *op.cit.*
11. A valuable source of details such as these is to be found in the annual reports produced by the Colonial (and later Commonwealth) Office, published by Her Majesty's Stationery Office in London.
12. James Cameron, foreign correspondent for the *Daily Express*, on a visit from London in 1949. See Deryck Scarr (2000). *Seychelles Since 1770: History of a slave and post-slavery society.* London: C. Hurst, p.152.
13. *Ibid.*
14. Commonwealth Office (1968). *Seychelles: Report for the years 1965 and 1966.* London: HMSO, p.21.
15. 'How has the world changed in the last 20 years?' United Nations Population Fund, 7 April 2014.

https://www.unfpa.org/news/how-has-world-changed-last-20-years (accessed 23 May 2018).

16 *Apocrypha*, 1 Esdras 4:41.
17 Sawkut Rojid, Ahmed Afif and Emilio Sacerdoti (June 2013). *Seychelles: How Classic Policies Restored Sustainability*. World Bank. Washington DC: World Bank.
18 The Seychelles version of Creole is closely aligned to French: hence *napa* is derived from *n'ya pas* meaning 'there is nothing'.
19 The IMF (International Monetary Fund) and the World Bank have complementary interests, the former to ensure realistic exchange rates and the latter to promote policies to eradicate poverty.
20 Rojid *et al, op.cit.*, p.viii. *Leve debrouye* can be translated as 'Get up and fend for yourself!'
21 For this advice I was indebted to Lise Bastienne, who was rightly convinced that this step was necessary.
22 Rojid, *et al, op.cit.*, p.ix.
23 'Welcome to Seychelles'. Lonely Planet. https://www.lonelyplanet com/seychelles (accessed 30 July 2018).
24 World Commission on Environment and Development (1987). *Our Common Future*, popularly known as the Bruntland Report. New York: United Nations.
25 Website of the Ministry of Environment, Energy and Climate Change, Seychelles. http://www.meecc.gov.sc/index.php/what-we-do/biodiversity/(accessed 30 July 2018).
26 World Guides: *Seychelles National Parks and Nature Reserves*. http://www.world-guides.com/africa/seychelles/seychelles_nation al_parks.html (accessed 30 July 2018).
27 National Day Address, 2016. State House, Seychelles.
28 I have written more fully about the Blue Economy, and my own role in helping to promote the concept, in my book: James Alix Michel (2016). *Rethinking the Oceans: Towards the Blue Economy*, published by Paragon House, St. Paul, Minnesota, USA.
29 In my introduction to *The Blue Economy: Seychelles' Vision of the*

Blue Economy. Seychelles: Ministry of Foreign Affairs, 2014.
30   The term, Blue Economy, had already been coined by Gunter Pauli, a Belgian economist and business innovator, although the meaning he gave to it was rather different from the more generic interpretation that has gained international currency.
31   United Nations (2012). https://sustainabledevelopment.un.org/content/.../2978BEconcept.pdf.
32   Michel (2016), *op.cit.*
33   An interview on the French television channel, France24, 14 December 2014.   http://www.seychellesnewsagency.com/articles/1955/The+world+must+do+something+about+climate+change%2C+says+Seychelles+President+to+France (accessed 16 July 2018).
34   James Michel (2014). *Island Nation in a Global Sea: Making the New Seychelles*. Seychelles: Office of the President, p.34
35   http://www.statehouse.gov.sc/uploads/downloads/filepath_54.pdf.
36   Extracts from the president's address on the occasion of the inauguration of the University of Seychelles, 29 November 2010.
37   *Ibid.*
38   *Ibid*, p.34.
39   *Ibid*, p.118.
40   Michel (2014), *op.cit.*, p.264.
41   Christian Bueger and Anders Wivel (2018). 'How do small island states maximize influence? Creole diplomacy and the smart state foreign policy of Seychelles', *Journal of the Indian Ocean Region*, Vol. 14, No. 2, p.170.
42   The French also possessed part of this territory but that is no longer part of the modern state of Somalia, having the status, instead, of an independent nation, Djibouti.
43   Jade Lindley (2016). *Somali Piracy: A Criminological Perspective*, Preface. Farnham, England: Ashgate Publishing.
44   Michel (2014), *op.cit.*, p.56.
45   *Ibid*, p.62.

46 'Contact Group on Piracy off the Coast of Somalia', Bureau of Political-Military Affairs, 20 January 2017. https://www.state.gov/t/pm/rls/fs/2017/266864.htm (accessed 31 July 2018).
47 The first observation is attributed to Tor Sellström, in his book, *Africa in the Indian Ocean: Islands in Ebb and Flow*, cited in the second article, namely, Bueger and Wivel, *op.cit.*, pp.170-188.
48 Bueger and Wivel, *op.cit.*, p.179.
49 Jean-Paul Adam, quoted in Bueger and Wivel, *op.cit.*
50 E.F. Schumacher (1973). *Small is Beautiful: Economics as if People Mattered*, Chapter 5, 'A Question of Size'. London: Blond & Briggs.
51 Michel (2014), *op.cit.*
52 Climate Policy Observer (2019). 'Alliance of Small Island States (AOSIS). http://climateobserver.org/country- profiles/alliance-of-small-island-states/ (accessed 15 January 2019).
53 This body was formally established by the United Nations General Assembly in 2001 although the UN's interest in SIDS had been previously highlighted at the Rio Earth Summit in 1992 and codified in 1994 as the Barbados Programme of Action.
54 Joana Nicette and Sharon Meriton-Jean, 'Small island states meet in Seychelles to agree on unified stance ahead of climate talks in Lima', 11 November 2014. http://www.seychellesnewsagency.com/articles/1752/Small+island+states+meet+in+Seychelles+to+agree+on+unified+stance+ahead+of+climate+talks+in+Lima (accessed 31 July 2018).
55 https://sidsgbn.org/ (accessed 22 March 2019).
56 Albert Einstein. It is believed that this is a variant of: 'a new type of thinking is essential if mankind is to survive and move toward higher levels', in an article in the New York Times, 25 May 1946.
57 Michel (2014), *op.cit., p.18.*
58 'A Moment with the President', Antoine Onezime in conversation with President Michel, 29 April 2009, State House Press Room, Seychelles.
59 Statistics are drawn from a variety of sources: The National

NOTES AND REFERENCES 217

Bureau of Statistics, Seychelles; World Health Organisation; and Commonwealth Health Online.
60 *Corinthians*, 13:12, King James Version.
61 G.K. Chesterton (1908). *The Secret People*, poem.
62 Nelson Mandela, as always perceptive, reminding us not only that we are responsible for our own actions but that these can never be divorced from one's inner being.
63 Olaf Palme, former Prime Minister of Sweden. In spite of – or probably because of – his unyielding views on freedom, in domestic as well international politics, Palme was assassinated in 1986. The assassin has never been found.
64 State of the Nation Address, February 2016.
65 *Daily Nation* (Kenya), 'Seychelles' President Michel surprised all when he announced his resignation', 1 October 2016. https://www.nation.co.ke/news/africa/seychelles-predident-michel-surprised-when-announced-resignation/1066-3401630-nivorb/index.html (accessed 12 January 2018).
66 http://www.statehouse.gov.sc/speeches.php?news_id=3142 (accessed 22 April 2019).
67 Composite dictionary definition.
68 Brian Aldiss, quoted by Michael Bishop in *The Washington Post*, 23 March 1980.
69 http://www.statehouse.gov.sc/speeches.php?news_id=3142 (accessed 22 April 2019).
70 Constitution of the Third Republic of Seychelles.
71 John Constable, *Youth*, 1898.
72 William Shakespeare, *The Rape of Lucrece*, poem 1794.
73 'What was President René's private phone number doing on dead drug dealer in America?' http://www.seychellesweekly.com/may_16_2008/page9.html (accessed 25 March 2019).
74 Ashton Robinson, 'Seychelles: at sea managing intelligence', *Journal of the Indian Ocean Region*, Vol.14, No.3, pp.331-342.
75 Speaker in the audience (who claimed to be a journalist) at the

conference in Abu Dhabi organized by *The Economist*, March 2019.
76 James R. Mancham (2014). *Seychelles: The saga of a small nation navigating the cross-currents of a big world*. St. Louis, Minnesota: Paragon Press, p.152.
77 *Ibid*, p.149.
78 *Matthew*, 26:8
79 *Corinthians*, 13:12, King James Version.
80 *Ephesians*, 25.
81 Ken Sinclair, 'Covid-19 new normal is not normal', 28 May 2020. https://www.contractormag.com/iot/article/21132496/covid19-new-normal-is-not-normal
82 United Nations (2020). https://www.un.org/en/sections/isues-depth/climate-change/
83 'World population by year', Worldometers. https:///www.worldometers.info/world-population/world-Population-by-year/ See also Tim Fox, 'Population growth: the defining challenge of the 21st century', *NATO Review*, February 2011. https://www.nato.int/docu/review/articles/2011/02/14/population-growth-the-defining-challenge-of-the-21st-century/index.html
84 Oliver Millman, 'Earth has lost a third of arable land in past 40 years, scientists say', *The Guardian*, 2 December 2015. Article based on a report produced by the Grantham Centre for Sustainable Futures, University of Sheffield. https://www.theguardian.com/environment/2015/dec/02/arable-land-soil-food-security-shortage
85 https://www.nationalgeographic.com/science/2020/04/experts-warned-pandemic-decades-ago-why-not-ready-for-coronavirus/
86 https://www.ajc.com/news/obama-warned-pandemic-threat-2014-but-republicans-blocked-funding/dh2H9HxiuBY05T5uPqtqpI/
87 https://www.worldometers.info/coronavirus/country/us/
88 Robert Harris (2009). *Pompeii*. London: Arrow Books, Penguin Random House.

89 UN Environment Programme (UNEP) Annual Report 2019. https://www.unenvironment.org/annualreport/2019/index.php
90 David Brower, recalling an assertion in a Sierra Club publication in 1956, in his Foreword, p.xiii, to Ehrlich, P.R., *The Population Bomb*. New York, Ballantine Books.
91 Joseph J. Bish, 'Population growth in Africa: grasping the scale of the challenge', *The Guardian*, 11 January 2016. https://www.theguardian.com/global-development-professionals-network/2016/jan/11/population-growth-in-africa-grasping-the-scale-of-the-challenge
92 The excerpt was taken from Carl Sagan's book, *Pale Blue Dot*, inspired by an image taken, at Sagan's suggestion, by Voyager 1 on 14 February 1990. https://www.planetary.org/worlds/pale-blue-dot
93 William Wordsworth (1850). *The Prelude,* bk.xi, 1.140.
94 'Bhutan's Gross National Happiness Index', *Oxford Poverty and Human Development Initiative*. https://ophi.org.uk/policy/national-policy/gross-national-happiness-index/ (accessed 10 April 2019).
95 *Ibid.*
96 In an interview with Robin Hammond of National Geographic, following my Blue Economy leadership award in Washington, June 2019.
97 John Dryden (1691). *Song of Venus*.
98 Eliot, T.S. (1944). *The Four Quartets*. London: Faber and Faber.

www.ingramcontent.com/pod-product-compliance
Lightning Source LLC
Chambersburg PA
CBHW040927240426
43667CB00024B/2976